THE ART OF RELEVANCE

Open new doors
and matter more!

ALSO BY NINA SIMON

The Participatory Museum

THE ART OF RELEVANCE

BY NINA SIMON

2016

ISBN: 978-0692701492
Published by Museum 2.0 Santa Cruz, California

TABLE OF CONTENTS

PART 5: THE HEART OF RELEVANCE

THE ART OF RELEVANCE

PREFACE BY JON MOSCONE

Let's face it: we have a problem. It's not that we don't see the numbers declining, or the funding priorities shifting, or the world passing us by. The problem is: what do we do?

This problem is a question of relevance, and it is a question that drives me in every way. When I became artistic director of California Shakespeare Theater in the Bay Area in 2000, I was really fresh. I promised the Board of Trustees that I could never deliver excellence, but that I could deliver passion and the attempt at authenticity. And I did. I believed, and still do, that we tell our own stories when we tell the stories of Shakespeare and other classic writers. It is through our personal lenses that we read, interpret, and communicate the words. I gave the stage to artists who had bold personal stories to communicate.

It worked. Cal Shakes mattered a lot to the people it mattered to. Our subscription renewal rates were always about 15% higher than the national average. People came back, and they told their friends to come.

And then at one point, I saw that despite all the success we had earned with the constituencies we held close, despite the open doors we held for so many people, we had almost zero relevance to communities of color. Individuals yes, but communities, no. Not on terms other than those we had proscribed. So we tried to make a new promise to matter more to more people. We ventured to find out if we could mean anything to people in Oakland through an engagement process around a new play to be written locating Hamlet's Elsinore in the kingdom of drugs that ravaged so many people and so much of a city in the late 1980s.

We owned our lack of credibility in these new communities. We partnered wisely, listened more than we talked, and brought new people close into the process of writing and performing the piece. It premiered in 2006 at San Francisco's Intersection for the Arts and its resident company, Campo Santo. We cracked open a door to classical theater that was invisible, and therefore impossible to find, for people who had never set foot in our space.

Yet after that, they still didn't. We didn't make good on the promise that Cal Shakes was going to include stories that mattered to more people. That was the new promise I made, and I had a hard time making good on it.

We tried, moved forward, and fell back. We stood by the door unsure how wide open it should swing. In 2009, Cal Shakes presented a play by a black author, Zora Neale Hurston, Spunk, that brought the Harlem Renaissance to the hills of Orinda, California. It was a big hit critically and with audiences, many new to our venue. Once a year, we produced a play specifically for audiences of color, and we began to crack open new relationships, new conversations, and new relevance. Then, in 2011, we presented a Shakespeare play, The Winter's Tale, directed by and cast entirely with artists of color. Our longtime audience rebelled. It broke open a new conversation with key stakeholders and board members, who saw the shift in relevance away from them.

On the surface, programming Shakespeare the way I did may looked like a typical move for a typical theater to attract an audience (and perhaps funders) it had decided it should/needed to/desired to reach. Which made it not groundbreaking in the least. But deep down there was something more happening. A current way underground the surface of our stage had been tapped, and a nerve had been hit. I found myself in conversations about race and privilege I never thought I'd have. My belief in giving artists the space to tell their stories through Shakespeare was put to a new test, not by the artists, or by myself, but by a shifting audience.

I had to work anew to bring longtime supporters along as we started mattering more to new people. We were no longer just relevant to our culturally upbeat, politically engaged, educated and mostly white audience—we in fact took a risk in losing some of that relevance. For some, I broke a promise I didn't even know I made.

When I figured this out, and I saw how far we had to go, and what a beautiful, necessary and difficult journey it was going to be, I knew it was time to pass the baton to someone smarter about all this and as fresh as I was the day I got there 15 years before.

The challenge of relevance is complex and deep. Even though my focus has now shifted—to turning art into civic action at the Yerba Buena Center for the Arts—the challenge remains the same. How to make honest promises to new people—and keep them. The journey to unlock the doors of our great big institution to let people in to experience and participate in work that matters to them has made me even more alive to the question of relevance than I ever thought possible.

All of us in the world of service—art, culture, religion, spirituality, community—our work has meaning. Relevance enables us to ignite and reignite that meaning. Relevance helps us find the key to unlock people's desire for it, and it gives them reasons to come in and partner with us.

If you are looking into the space of meaning and wondering why you can't get in, or looking out onto the street from that space and wondering why they are not coming, then this is the book that you must read, right now, and maybe twice.

This book will bring power to your struggle for relevance. It won't solve your problems for you. It will help you figure out how to be alive to the question of relevance and meaning in your work. Which is the surest route, I believe, to find answers.

INTRODUCTION: UNLOCKING RELEVANCE

When the Japanese-American family walked into the tiny museum at Camp Amache in 2010, graduate student Kellen Hinrichsen was there to greet them. Kellen welcomed the group: an older man, his daughter, and grandchildren. The grandfather was born at Camp Amache, one of many children born in captivity in the World War II internment camps. Kellen showed the family around the museum, highlighting displays related to childhood in the camps. The old man seemed to enjoy himself as he and his family perused the museum. But his tone was somber. He told Kellen that he had no paperwork from his birth at the camp hospital: no intake paperwork, no birth records, not even an original birth certificate. All the files had been lost when the camps were hastily shut down.

Kellen realized that the museum might be able to help. Deep in the archives of the tiny museum were stacks of newspapers printed in the internment camp. Kellen asked for the man's birth date and searched the newspaper database. Nothing on that day mentioned the man's birth. Nor the day after. They checked one more paper, and there, two days after his birthday, they found his birth announcement.

They found it. For the first time, the man had written proof of his birth. The museum unlocked something of value, something he had been seeking his whole life. He cried. His family cried. Kellen cried. They took photos of the newspaper announcement and another one about a woman born on the same day (the man hoped to track her down). They thanked Kellen, took one last look around, and left.

Those newspapers sat in boxes for years. Many people might have asked why they were relevant to anyone at all. But for the right people, those newspapers were priceless. They were the key: to family, to identity, to existence.

This is a beautiful story. It's the kind of story that inspired me to start writing this book. And I know it's not the only story of its kind. If you work in a place of passion and public service, you probably have a story like Kellen's. The teenager who found his calling in your state park. The immigrant who first registered to vote at your library. The prisoner who felt a little freer through your theater program. That girl who found purpose in a poem. Heck, you yourself may be driven in your work because of a transformative experience that opened a door for you, long ago.

Here's what fascinates and frustrates me about these stories: they are not enough. If your work lives in a locked room with a tiny door, with only a few keys out in circulation to open it, few people will know. Few people will care. It doesn't matter how powerful the experience is inside the room if most people cannot or choose not to enter.

Those internment camp newspapers mattered to Kellen as a professional. They mattered to the Japanese-American family as an essential piece of personal information. To nearly everyone else, they weren't relevant at all.

And "everyone else" often includes the people making decisions about funding and societal value. To succeed, we need to expand our value—and not just for the individuals to whom we are already relevant. We need to matter more to more people if we want our work to shine.

To me, mattering more is a question of relevance. I've spent the past five years leading the Santa Cruz Museum of Art & History—the MAH—through a resurgence of community involvement. When I arrived in 2011, the Board of Trustees was considering closing its doors. The MAH didn't matter enough to enough people, or to the right people, to succeed. Most of the community didn't even know it existed. Like so many of my colleagues in museums and libraries, theaters and universities, parks and churches, we struggled to answer the question: "Are you even relevant anymore?" with a resounding "YES." YES to funders, YES to politicians, YES to potential visitors and learners and creators and lovers.

And so we sought, little by little, to understand what mattered to people in our community. To understand how we could replace our locked doors with ones that opened widely to our community and the cultural experiences they sought. We started experimenting, changing, and expanding our audiences and offerings. We did so flying a flag of relevance.

At the time, I defined relevant experiences as those connected to the needs, assets, and interests of our community, and to the art and history in our collection. But over time I started to feel uncertain about this definition. I started to wonder if just making "connections" was enough. Every time a marketing guru described relevance in terms of cultural trends, I felt uneasy. Were we pandering at my museum when we offered people content related to their own experiences? Were we splashing a superficial coat of paint over museum traditions to motivate people to attend? I didn't think we were doing that—but I also didn't have other language or tools to define what we were doing.

These goals sent me on an exploratory mission to understand relevance: what it is, what it isn't, how it works, why it matters. I sought out stories like Kellen's, so I could dissect them, learn from them, and share them with you. These stories aren't just about someone making a link to an institution. They are about making connections that unlock meaning. That's what I want to do. And I want to do it with more people—with people with different backgrounds and perspectives, people who might not think they could derive any meaning from a museum at all.

The stories in this book are my field notes from this journey. They are peppered with theory and surprising conclusions along the way. I hope these stories deepen your own desire to pursue relevance in your work, unlocking meaning and value for diverse people in your community.

While this mission awakened my appreciation for relevance, it also made me more aware of its limitations. Relevance is a paradox. It is essential; it gets people to pay attention, to walk in the door, to open their hearts. But it is also meaningless without powerful programming on the other side of the door. If the door doesn't lead to valuable offerings, if nothing touches peoples' hearts, interest fades. They don't return.

This is a book about the paradox of relevance. I do not believe that relevance is the panacea of audience development, a virtue above all others. I believe relevance unlocks new ways to build deep connections with people who don't immediately self-identify with our work. I believe relevance is the key to a locked room where meaning lives. We just have to find the right keys, the right doors, and the humility and courage to open them.

WHAT IS RELEVANCE?

Relevance is a key that unlocks meaning.

It opens doors to experiences that matter to us,
surprise us, and bring value into our lives.

A WALK ON THE BEACH

On the morning of July 19, 2015, I pedaled my bike downhill towards certain failure. It was a Sunday, 7:30am and chilly. I was headed to the beach. My museum—the MAH—was holding a 130th anniversary party for the first surfers in the Americas. On July 19, 1885, three teenage Hawaiian princes put on the first surfing demonstration ever documented on the mainland of North America in Santa Cruz, California. 130 years later to the day, we went to the same beach to honor the princes' legacy with a surfing demo on replicas of their original redwood boards.

This all sounds nice on paper. But it also sounds like the stuff of every poorly thought-out grasp for relevance. Surfing is huge in Santa Cruz, but our museum was celebrating an anniversary no one knew about, at a time of year when the waves are dead. At a time of day when most people are sleeping. Tied to a museum exhibition few had seen. Anchored by two ancient hunks of wood—those very first Santa Cruz redwood surfboards, on loan from the Bishop Museum in Hawaii for a homecoming tour at our museum.

As I locked up my bike, I steeled myself for minor embarrassment. I prayed there'd be a few dozen people at the beach, a couple surfers on the replica surfboards. I'd be a good museum director, say a few words, and we'd call it a day. Hopefully, there'd be enough friends and family to pat ourselves on the back and say we did something good for history.

I was wrong. I arrived at the beach to the biggest crowd I've ever seen at 8am. I stumbled towards the hushed throng, heads bent before a blessing of the boards by a Hawaiian elder. Legendary big wave surfers shook my hand. Someone put a lei around my neck. I walked with hundreds of fellow Santa Cruzans along the shoreline to watch professional surfers attempt to ride the replicas. We lined the base of the cliffs like barnacles. Crowds formed on the sidewalks above the cliff edges, cameras hanging over the fence. The tide was low, the sun came out, and we walked way out along the break, water swirling around our shins, cheering the surfers on, watching them rise and fall.

Back on the beach, the mayor proclaimed it Three Princes Day. Members of a Polynesian motorcycle club—a fierce pack of muscle and leather in a sea of sand and flowers—hefted the replica surfboards and carried them down the beach, like a reverse funeral for history being raised from the dead. At the river mouth where the princes first surfed in 1885, Hawaiian elders led us in a song of blessing. And then we got into the water again—hundreds of us, on replica redwood boards and longboards and shortboards and paddleboards and no boards at all, paddling out to form a circle in the ocean beyond the break. We raised our arms together and splashed in joy. We paddled back, dried off, and spent the afternoon drinking beer and dancing hula in the courtyard outside the museum.

The Princes of Surf project changed my work. It smashed museum attendance records, garnered oceans of press, and shattered my pre-conceptions about who connects with history and how. Grown men fought for standing room at lectures about the history of the boards. Couples stopped me on the street to marvel about the princes. Kids wore commemorative t-shirts around town. Grizzled surfers pulled me aside to ask if we could swap out the real boards for replicas, keep the originals, and send the replicas back to Hawaii instead.

Princes of Surf changed my life personally, too. It turned me into a surfer. It opened up a new side of Santa Cruz to me. It made me wonder: what is relevance?

I'd always seen relevance as a link, a piece of connective tissue linking someone to something. If something was relevant to you, I figured, it meant that it mattered to you.

Clearly, Princes of Surf mattered to a lot of people in Santa Cruz. But here's the thing: a lot of the work we did at my museum was linked to local interests. Many of our exhibitions seemed just as connected to what it means to be a Santa Cruzan as Princes of Surf. What made this exhibition different? Was it just about numbers—more people feeling that link than was typical? Or was something else going on?

When I looked into the research on relevance, I discovered that experts define relevance as more than a link. In the words of cognitive scientists Deirdre Wilson and Dan Sperber, relevance "yields positive cognitive effect." Something is relevant if it gives you new information, if it adds meaning to your life, if it makes a difference to you. It's not enough for something to be familiar, or connected to something you already know. Relevance leads you somewhere. It brings new value to the table.

In other words, it's not enough to say: Santa Cruzans like surfing, ergo, they will like a surfing exhibit. Sure, they'll like it. But will it give them something new? Something that matters? That's what makes it relevant.

And so, instead of thinking of relevance as a link, I started thinking of relevance as a key. Imagine a locked door. Behind the door is a room that holds something powerful—information, emotion, experience, value. The room is dazzling. The room is locked.

Relevance is the key to that door. Without it, you can't experience the magic that room has to offer. With it, you can enter. The power of relevance is not how connected that room is to what you already know. The power is in the experiences the room offers... and how wonderful it feels to open the door and walk inside.

When I thought of relevance as a key, my understanding of Princes of Surf changed. Princes of Surf wasn't just an exhibition about surfing. It was an exhibition that confirmed an apocryphal origin story about Santa Cruz and surfing in the Americas. The whole project started years before the exhibition, when a gang of surf historians discovered those 1885 Santa Cruzan surfboards in storage at the Bishop Museum in Hawaii. I remember the phone call when they asked if the museum would support their research. I can still see those sunburnt surfers sitting in my office, speaking in hushed tones about "Project X." Their discovery was so fresh, so explosive, so tenuous that they didn't want to name it out loud.

Their research checked out. The story was true, the boards were real, and we worked hard to bring them home. The artifacts we displayed in Princes of Surf—those two simple redwood slabs—are like the Shroud of Turin of surfing in the Americas. They are proof that Hawaiians brought surfing to Santa Cruz first.

That connection matters to Santa Cruz. It fulfilled a deep desire for community identity and meaning. It unlocked a new door to understanding ourselves. Those boards whisper to Santa Cruz, you are part of something greater than yourselves: across oceans, across cultures, across time. It's not about nostalgia. It's about unlocking a new connection to something deep inside.

Princes of Surf is simple. It started with a theme—surfing—connected to our community. It started with a community—surfers—who were invested in unlocking deeper meaning around their passion. And then, it delivered something relevant: something new and shocking, old and reverent, something we were hungry for in our hearts.

Relevance is only valuable if it opens a door to something valuable. Once I understood the depth of Princes of Surf, I got embarrassed thinking about all the other projects I thought were relevant, doorways I had built for rooms that were hardly more than stage sets. Too often, our work opens doors to shallow, interchangeable rooms. We adorn the entrances with phrases like FUN! or FOR YOU!, but that doesn't change what's behind the doors. We lie to ourselves, writing shiny press releases for second-class objects and secondhand stories. The rechewed meat of culture. We tell ourselves that as long as we link our work to people's interests on the surface, they'll be rushing for our door.

And they may come in the door... but they won't come back. Doors to dullness are quickly forgotten. They give culture a bad name. Relevance only leads to deep meaning if it leads to something substantive. Killer content. Unspoken dreams. Memorable experiences. Muscle and bone.

So let's celebrate relevance. Not as an end, but a means. Because relevance is just a start. It is a key. You've got to get people in the door. But what matters most is the glorious experience they're moving towards, on the other side.

MEANING, EFFORT, BACON

In pop culture land, relevance is all about now. Who's hot. What's trending.

But if you're like me, that definition is deeply unsatisfying. And the experts are on our side. Remember Deirdre Wilson & Dan Sperber—the cognitive scientists who described relevance as something that "yields positive cognitive effect"? They are leading theorists in the study of relevance. And their definition of relevance is more complex—and useful—than simply what's hot.

Deirdre and Dan study how we transmit and receive information, mostly through speech. They argue that there are two criteria that make information relevant:

1. How likely that new information is to stimulate a **positive cognitive effect**—to yield new conclusions that matter to you.

2. How much **effort** is required to obtain and absorb that new information. The lower the effort, the higher the relevance.

These two criteria for relevance apply to all the stories in this book. Think about Kellen and the Japanese-American family. The museum was linked to the experience of the grandfather in the family, but it was the newspaper that unlocked new value and meaning. Not every newspaper in the collection was relevant; only the one that had the birth announcement generated the "positive cognitive effect." It was the right key for that family's emotional connection.

That key was hard to find, but not impossible. If those newspapers hadn't been indexed, or if it had taken days to find the right one, the family and Kellen might not have bothered. The effort was manageable. They found the key and turned the lock.

These criteria for relevance apply to both extraordinary and everyday experiences. Imagine you are considering going out to see a movie. You start seeking relevant information. You read a review that gets you excited about a particular film (a positive cognitive effect). You feel confident you'll enjoy that movie. If it's playing at convenient times at a theater nearby (low effort), you're set. You buy a ticket.

But if the movie is not showing nearby (high effort), or the reviews you read are conflicting and full of muddled information (negative cognitive effect), you're stuck. You don't get the useful conclusions you seek. It takes too much effort to find the right key to the door. You stay home.

Fulfilling these two criteria well can make a huge difference in how people respond to information. I saw this in 2015, when the World Health Organization released a study showing that processed meats— like bacon, ham, and sausages—are among the top five most cancerous products, alongside established killers like cigarettes and asbestos.

When I first saw this news, I was nonplussed. My husband and I are vegetarians, and for years, we've been reading studies like this. Top international health organizations have claimed for decades that a meat-free diet is vital to human health (not to mention reducing climate change impact). Period.

I assumed this 2015 study would have the same impact as all the others. Vegetarians and vegans would pass them around. We'd hesitantly foist them on our meat-eating friends and family members, expecting a mixture of disinterest, disbelief, and derision. And then everyone would go back to eating what they eat, believing what they believe.

But the 2015 study was different. It blew up on Facebook. It spawned thousands of news pieces, not just on health and foodie sites, but also on news outlets high and low. National papers. Business pages. Tech magazines. Op-eds. Blogs.

I walked into the dentist's office a week after the study came out, and the hygienist who cleaned my teeth told me the story had inspired her and her teenage son to stop eating meat. Here I'd spent years fumbling to get people who love me to even discuss the impact of eating meat, and one press release had motivated her family to give it up entirely.

I was blown away. How could one study—showing exactly what many other prominent studies have shown—have so much impact?

Consider the 2015 study in the context of relevance theory. The study linked two things that mattered to Americans in 2015: bacon and cancer. These are both emotionally-loaded topics. As a nation, we love bacon and eat it whenever we can. We hate cancer and avoid it however we can.

When a study links something we love to something we hate, it yields a conclusion that matters to us. The first criterion for relevance is satisfied. The research creates a surprising new connection between two things we care about. The mouthwatering sizzle of bacon on a pan. The pain we felt when our aunt went through chemo. It's impossible not to experience a "cognitive effect" when reading about it—whether it yields a conclusion of distress, resolve to change, or somewhere in between. The effect may not be "positive" in how it feels, but it is "positive" in that it adds information to the decisions at hand.

You could argue that any study about the health impacts of food is relevant to all of us. After all, we all eat. But that relevance is only meaningful if it yields a conclusion that matters to you. And if bacon suddenly tastes like the pain of your aunt dying of cancer… that matters.

Throw cigarettes into the story and you satisfy the second criterion for relevance. This study's conclusions were easy to understand. It took very little effort to connect the dots between our past experiences as a nation with cigarettes and new implications about bacon. Americans used to love cigarettes, until we discovered they cause cancer. Now, for the most part, we hate cigarettes. Does this mean we will one day feel about bacon the way we feel about cigarettes? Will little kids throw away their parents' processed meat, crying that they don't want to see Daddy die?

I hope so. But I suspect that the effort required to act on these conclusions will be too great for many bacon-lovers. There may be people like my dental hygienist out there, making a big effort based on the conclusions she has made. But there will be others who accept the information (the positive cognitive effect) but not the effort required to act.

If we want our work to be relevant, we need to satisfy both criteria. We need to provide a positive cognitive effect, and we need to make it possible with minimal effort. How likely is someone to derive a positive cognitive effect from visiting your site? How much effort will it require for them to do so? If it's easy to visit, and the experience yields value, your work is bound to be relevant. But if it's difficult to visit, and the value of the experience is hard to describe, why would anybody care to try?

SOMETHING OLD, SOMETHING NEW

It's late at night, and you're looking for something to watch on TV. Do you choose the movie you've seen before or a new one you know nothing about?

For most people, each of these is appealing for different reasons. Novelty is exciting, but risky. Familiarity is comforting, but redundant. We all want some of each in our lives.

One of the biggest critiques about relevance is that it's all about familiarity. Critics argue that relevance means dumbing down information, only giving people "what they want." These critics are worried that, if given the choice, we will always chose to consume information related to what we already know. We'll never open our eyes to anything new. We will stay trapped in the narrow swim lane of our own experience within a vast ocean of possibilities.

And yet we swim outside the lane again and again. The argument equating relevance with familiarity is overly simplistic. It ignores the reality that we all try something new once in awhile. Most of us do it with eagerness and pleasure—not pain. So what differentiates the circumstances where we choose familiarity and those where we choose novelty? How does relevance fit into these decisions?

Relevance theorists argue that the fundamental nature of relevance is not about familiarity. It is not about connecting something new with information you already have. It's about how likely that new information is to yield conclusions that matter to you. To answer a question on your mind. To confirm a suspicion. To fulfill a dream. To set your path forward.

But remember the other piece of relevance theory: relevance is inversely correlated with effort. The harder something is to understand or connect with, the less relevant it will seem. And here's where familiarity shines: it significantly reduces effort. When you've done something before, you've already made the connection. It's much, much easier to do it again. Familiarity encourages cycles of repetition. It offers alternatives to the effort and risk involved in trying new things.

We may not crave familiarity, but we settle on it as a safe way to generate a reasonable amount of satisfaction. We go back to that restaurant. We read another novel by the same author. However, when we identify something new that could bring meaning into our lives without a whole lot of effort, we take the leap. We desire relevance, and we're willing to take a risk and do some work to get it.

That's why so many successful stories of relevance cloak something novel in something familiar. When the New World Symphony in Miami wanted to connect younger, urban residents with classical music, they created a new language for their concerts. They presented outdoor "wallcast" productions, pairing visual art projections with live orchestral performances. Their marketing staff headed down to South Beach on the weekend to hand out "day of" advertisements for symphonic concerts alongside marketers pushing flyers for clubs and bars. The concert content was classical, but their form spoke the language of their urban, hip community. They tied something novel for young adults—live orchestral music—to more familiar experiences.

The Symphony didn't change the music to reach new people. They changed the way young people saw classical music concerts, helping new audiences perceive the symphony as a relevant, compelling way to spend a Saturday night.

This change was not something most young adults could achieve on their own. For people unfamiliar with orchestral performances, it takes too many leaps of imagination—too much effort—for most people to decide that the symphony could fulfill desires for stimulation, social connection, and artistic pleasure. The New World Symphony had to do the work to create the relevance, reduce the effort, connect the novel to the familiar, and help people open themselves to new, hopefully positive experiences.

Too often, we expect people to do the work of manufacturing relevance on their own. They won't. It's too much work. Our brains crave efficiency. If it takes too many leaps to get from here to there, relevance goes down. The line need not be straight, but it must be clear, and short.

Imagine you are someone who yearns to live a creative life. Both a craft night and a theatrical production are relevant to your interests. They could each bring meaning to your life. But the craft night is free and the theater tickets are expensive. The craft night is at a friend's house where you've been before and the theater is in an unfamiliar part of town. You can wear jeans to craft night; who knows what you wear to the theater? You weigh the options, and from an effort perspective, the choice is clear. You go to craft night.

Does that mean the theater is irrelevant to your interests? Not at all. It just takes too much effort to get to the point where your butt is in a seat.

Relevance isn't about what you already know. It's about what you'd like to know, where you'd like to go, and what experiences you think will help you get there. Ice hockey star Wayne Gretzky was famous for saying "I skate to where the puck is going." Something is relevant when it is connected to where a person wants to go. What you want to know. Who you want to be.

But let's face it: dreaming big, skating to where the puck is going— that's hard work! It requires really knowing yourself, having a vision and goals for the future, and having some idea of the steps required to get there. It's much easier if the institution can meet you in the middle, reach out a hand, and invite you in.

Many cultural experiences are new to people. Many people have never visited a museum, climbed a volcano, or prayed in public before. The novelty of these experiences doesn't diminish the potential for these experiences to be relevant. They may be extremely relevant—to a person who wants to be an artist, wants to take on physical challenges, or wants a spiritual community. The challenge is not in the novelty but in the effort required to make a relevant connection. We have to help make the connection and reduce the effort. When we can do that, people will get off the couch and try something new.

TWO DELUSIONS ABOUT RELEVANCE

People who do important work often delude ourselves about relevance in two ways:

1. We believe what we do is relevant to everyone. We can connect it to everyday life, ergo, it is relevant. Everyone can see the door, everyone already has a key, and they can open the door anytime they like.

2. We believe that relevance is irrelevant, since people will be attracted to our work for its distinctiveness. It is NOT like everyday life, and that is the glorious point. There is no door, there is no key, there is only a magical experience to fall into like Alice through the looking glass.

Both of these are delusions. Let's pierce them one by one.

DELUSION #1: WHAT WE DO IS RELEVANT TO EVERYONE

This delusion is borne from the theory that we can't possibly be ir-relevant because our work is relevant to everyone. It sounds like this: "Shakespeare is relevant to everyone because it illuminates the human condition." Or this: "Climate science is relevant to everyone because we all live on this planet." Or this: "The word of God is relevant to everyone, whether they attend church or not."

Whether these statements are true or not is immaterial. You cannot assign relevance by fiat. People choose for themselves what is relevant. You can't dictate it from on high.

Nor, frankly, should you. Arguments for universal relevance are weak, even desperate. The more vociferously you argue for the relevance of your work, the more it implies fear that people believe otherwise. If you have to cry out, "History is relevant!," you're already losing.

You can't force a connection by argument alone.

Arguments for universal relevance are nearly impossible to win. Relevance is always relative. "Is it relevant?" is an incomplete question. The question is always: "WHO is it relevant to?" or "WHAT is it relevant to?"

If you love football, then a news story about last night's game is relevant to you. If you're a parent, a law changing local school district lines is relevant to you. If you're a Harley enthusiast, an exhibition on motorcycle design is relevant to you.

Relevance often functions in the binary. Information is relevant or irrelevant, the door unlocked or locked. The newspapers from the dates surrounding the Japanese-American man's birth were relevant to him. The other issues were just paper.

What is relevant to one person can be irrelevant to their neighbor. What's more, what is relevant today may be irrelevant tomorrow. Today, you care if your plane is delayed. Tomorrow, when you are enjoying your destination, the flight schedule no longer matters.

Occasionally relevance is linear. Information is more or less relevant, the door more or less open. Think about that law changing school district lines. If the law is being considered two counties over, you probably don't know or care much about it. If you don't have children, it's not even on your radar. But threaten to change the law in your district, for your kid who loves her first grade teacher with all her heart, and suddenly, the issue is relevant.

Relevance is relative even when it comes to the most commonly shared experiences. There are some people who will never watch the Super Bowl. There are some people who will never feel an impulse to spirituality. These people are not bad, wrong, or in need of fixing. They have found relevance in other pursuits.

The sooner we start focusing on becoming relevant to the people we most care about—as opposed to proclaiming our relevance to everyone—the more successful and powerful we will be.

It may be true that our work, or our issues, touch everyone. But that doesn't mean that they matter to everyone. Relevance is relative, and people are busy. Our work is only relevant when people tell us it is. When they feel connected to it. When they believe that it matters.

DELUSION #2: RELEVANCE IS IRRELEVANT

Maybe you are more drawn to an opposite delusion: the belief that relevance doesn't matter. That you don't need it to reach people. That people will discover the magic in your work without you reaching out to them and opening the door. That your work is so transformative, so awesome, that it doesn't have to be connected to the thrum of daily life.

I believe in this magic as much as anyone. When I was a child, I spent hours in the living room of my mother's house. It had floor-to-ceiling bookshelves packed with her books. She'd arranged them using her own system, partly thematic, partly alphabetical. I'd climb up on the back of the couch, my feet sinking into the cushions, running my fingers across their mysterious spines. When I hit twelve, I started picking books out, haphazardly. I found books that blew my mind. Tropic of Cancer, which taught me that swearing wasn't invented in my lifetime. Understanding Comics, which I consider one of the most important books on design I've ever read. Sex Tips for Girls, which my mom still can't believe I read when I was a kid.

None of these books were relevant to me. They were enticing because they were irrelevant to me. They were books of the adult world, mysterious and powerful. And a few of them changed my life.

This is the kind of story we often tell ourselves as an argument against pursuing relevance. That a visitor will wander into the Rothko room and be overwhelmed with the paintings' pulsing power. That someone will show up for an opera for the first time and get swept away by the richness. That a person will peek into a church and feel the word of God as true and unmistakable as a thunder clap.

And in a way, it's true. Many of our most powerful experiences are not rooted in relevance. The things that shock us, blow us away, or confound us—many of these things are unexpected. We aren't ushered in by relevance. We just slam into that tree, fall into that painting, lock eyes across a room and BAM—something new matters.

But lightning strikes are few and far between. Most of our days, most of our experiences—both important and mundane—are steered and filtered by what we deem relevant. Most of the books I read as a child were NOT the ones I pulled off my mom's shelves. Those were the rarities. I found many more life-changing books through relevant channels—school, age-appropriate book lists, friends' recommendations—than I did through the random mystique of her living room.

When you start looking more closely at lightning strike stories, the watermark of relevant doors and keyholes becomes visible. Someone had to drag that newbie to the opera. Something pulled that person up the church steps to the door. I only encountered those transportive adult books because they were in my own house. It doesn't get much more relevant than that.

Relevance determines most of what we do. The paths we walk. The choices we make. The things we read. The new things we try—or avoid trying. If we deem something relevant, we'll open that door. And sometimes it pays off by leading us somewhere important. Into a coffee shop that becomes a second home. Into an art form that sparks new ideas. Into a temple that becomes a spiritual haven. Into a relationship that changes our lives.

If you work for an organization that seeks to provide meaningful, powerful, significant experiences, you should care about being relevant. You probably already do. You care about opening the door of relevance to those powerful experiences. Don't rely on people walking in on their own and getting hit by lightning. Lightning strikes too infrequently. Our work is too important to wait.

A NOTE ON IRRELEVANCE

"That's irrelevant."

This sentence is sometimes used to imply that irrelevance is synonymous with triviality. If something is irrelevant, it doesn't matter. It's meaningless.

Not true. Irrelevance is a distraction, and a dangerous one.

Imagine walking up to two doors. One door is wood, locked, simple. It leads to the room you seek. The other is gold, dazzling, singing an irritating yet catchy tune. You open the dazzling door. You slam your head on the blank wall behind it. And now you're backing away, rubbing your head, wondering why you walked up to those damn doors in the first place.

Irrelevance can be dangerously distracting. It can draw us away from what we intended, what we desired, what we came here to do.

Irrelevance can be damaging, especially for organizations with limited resources to attract and engage people. Irrelevance is just as appealing to those of us doing the work as it is to those we seek to reach. Irrelevance is everywhere. It is in every sexy new technology. Every program pursued strictly to fulfill a funder's interest. Every short-sighted way that we get people's attention without capturing their imagination.

Irrelevance often cloaks itself in familiarity, feigning relevance. Irrelevant things often seem relevant to everyone. Free food. Sexual titillation. If you provide free food, people will come. If you integrate sexual innuendo into a church sign, people will read the sign.

But will they connect with whatever you actually wanted them to come for? Will it have meaning for them? The church service, the sales pitch, the exhibition opening?

Maybe not.

When I became director of the MAH, our busiest night of the

month was First Friday. We were regularly attracting 500 people to an evening of free exhibits, live music, and tasty appetizers. But we had a problem. People spent all their time dancing, eating, and socializing on the ground floor. Very few made it up the stairs to the exhibition galleries.

On one level, this wasn't a problem. It's good for people to have convivial experiences in a museum. But we wanted visitors to connect with exhibitions. We knew we had more to offer them if we could entice them upstairs.

So we did something counterintuitive: we cut the free food.

Free food was irrelevant to the museum. It wasn't making the museum matter more to people. It wasn't about art. It wasn't about history. It was about food. In addition to all its delicious, distracting qualities, free food was a literal barrier to people visiting the exhibitions, because they couldn't bring their plates into the galleries.

I'm a bit embarrassed to recall how nervous I was about cutting the food at First Friday. I had two fears. First, I was afraid people would be upset that we dropped something they loved. Second—and more importantly—I was afraid that people might stop coming. I was afraid the food was the only thing bringing them into the museum.

But we took the plunge. We cut the food. We added a hands-on art activity. Within months, attendance had doubled—and everyone was making the trek up the stairs to exhibitions. Within a year, attendance tripled. 1,500 people were coming monthly for an evening of exhibitions, live music, art activities… and no food.

It turned out that the food was not relevant. It was a distraction. It was a shiny barrier masquerading as a door. Right after we cut the food, there were a couple complaints. Within a few months, it was as if the free food had never existed. The event became more afford-able to present, more on-mission in its content, and more attractive to more people. Arguably, First Friday became more relevant—even as we eschewed one of the most appealing enticements we had to offer.

When I see a church with a sign outside that says "Sunday's Message: Jesus said, Bring me that ass" or "God's favorite word is Come,"* I smile. But I also know they are wasting their time. Sex may be attractive. It may be arresting. But unless it will help people make meaning at church, it's irrelevant.

*Yes, these are real.

OUTSIDE IN

There are two kinds of people in the world of relevance: outsiders and insiders.

Insiders are in the room. They know it, love it, protect it. Outsiders don't know your doors exist. They are uninterested, unsure, unwelcome.

If you want new people to come inside, you need to open new doors—doors that speak to outsiders— and welcome them in.

PEOPLE WHO DON'T NORMALLY SHOW UP

When Yosi Sergant was recruited by the Obama campaign in 2007 as a media consultant, he was told: "We're not going to win unless people who normally don't show up show up." It was his task to bring new people to the polls.

Yosi was new to politics, so he asked, "Where should I start?" They told him to go and get an endorsement from the Fresno Bee.

Yosi looked at his bosses in disbelief. He didn't know much about politics. But he knew something about young people. And he knew that the Fresno Bee's endorsement wouldn't mean squat to them.

Relevance is an exercise in empathy—understanding what matters to your intended audience, not what matters to you. Yosi's audience was people who have rarely voted historically: young people, people of color. They were outside the traditional world of politics. Maybe they saw the doors to enter. Maybe they didn't. For whatever reason, voting wasn't relevant to them.

Yosi knew that getting young people to the polls wasn't a matter of getting endorsements from newspapers or traditional "get out the vote" campaigns. He had to reach the right people, with the right message, delivered by the right messenger... a messenger trusted by the young urban adults he sought to reach.

The messenger he chose was Shepard Fairey. Shepard was a graffiti artist, skateboarder, and philosopher-king of the streets. He was a guerrilla activist, known for stylized posters of Andre the Giant with the word OBEY plastered menacingly across them. He operated way outside the Democratic establishment. Yosi ran into him at a party, where they chatted about their mutual admiration for Barack Obama. Yosi asked: "Do you think you could do something to help get him elected?" The next day, Shepard called, asking if the campaign might be open to a poster in a street art style. And the iconic HOPE image was born.

Yosi and Shepard orchestrated a series of events, images, and merchandise under the Manifest:Hope banner. Manifest:Hope was a movement, an art exhibition, a concert series, a t-shirt, a Facebook plugin. It was everything that spoke to the community they wanted to reach. It was the key to the door of a meaningful election, a candidate who gave people hope. Young people of color came. They saw. They bought. They voted.

Yosi couldn't drag young people to the polls. He couldn't tell them that Barack Obama was relevant. He could only present Obama to them in relevant terms.

START AT THE FRONT DOOR

People define for themselves what they value, and thus, what they deem relevant. But that doesn't mean relevance is a pure trait, fixed within each person's identity. You can make something relevant to anyone.

Imagine you're at a conference and you're about to split into breakout groups. Everyone counts off from one to four. When the count comes to you, you say, "three." Once everyone has counted, the facilitator says: "Ones go to the lobby. Twos head to the patio. Threes are in the auditorium. Fours head to the classroom."

Where do you go?

Immediately, you're on your way to the auditorium—or figuring out how to get there. You're looking around to see who else is a three. You're wondering what will happen when you get to the auditorium. Suddenly, all these things are relevant to you. In fact, it's probably a bit hard to even recall where those other people were assigned to go because you became focused on your particular task as a number three. All things "three" are now relevant to you. The other numbers are not.

We manufacture this kind of relevance for each other all the time, to positive and negative effect. On the positive side, you can make something relevant with an externality—even an arbitrary one. On the negative side, when someone thinks something isn't relevant to them (like all those other numbers), they completely block it out.

It's rare that someone tells you, "you are a three," but every day people tell you—directly and indirectly, correctly and incorrectly—who you are and what is relevant to you.

You're a boy; use this restroom.

You're black; do you play basketball?

You're overweight; you don't belong at this nightclub.

You're elderly; try the low-impact aerobics class.

You're Jewish; have you read this book about Israel?

Our differences are like individual keys crowding our key rings, bouncing around in our pockets. They open certain doors and not others.

We start with the keys we were given, by our parents, teachers, and peers. They are partly internally defined and partly determined by societal norms. These norms define what doors we see as appealing, or open to us, as we navigate potential experiences. This doesn't mean we can't transcend these categories and acquire new keys. We can and we do, every day. But we continue to carry the keys given to us, even if they're not the ones we would have chosen.

That's why so many bids for relevance start by appealing to the keys we already have. These are the front doors, the obvious ones. Harley exhibitions for motorcyclists. Pub science for engineers. African-American playwrights for Black History Month. Rock concerts for Christian youth. These first doors fit our keys. They call out: "Hey number threes! This one's for you."

If you're going to open new doors—especially doors to the heart— you have to start at the front door. You have to show that you are inviting people in on their terms, with generosity, humility, and a nod to what speaks to them. Effective front doors have greeters who look like your community welcoming them at the door. Speaking their language. Providing entry points that match the keys they use every day.

Opening that first door is important. But if you only engage at the front door, your relevance will be limited. If your institution wants to be relevant to Latino people, you can't do it once a year on Cinco de Mayo. If your institution wants to be relevant to young people, you can't do it with a marketing campaign alone.

Why not? Because the front door is only the introduction to the experience within. If a newcomer opens the door and has a lousy time in the room, or if she only feels welcome at specific times or events, she may start questioning the value of the key in her hand. Why did I think that experience would be relevant to me? Why didn't it yield the kind of meaning I had hoped for? If that Latina mom encounters enough uninspired, superficial cultural festivals, she may opt out in the future, no longer assuming they are relevant or valuable.

But if she walks through the door and the experience is brilliant, she'll keep the key. She walks out satisfied and appreciative of the institution as a place that offers satisfaction. She walks out curious about what else it can offer her.

The more you start to matter to people, the more they will desire opportunities to go deeper into the room of what you offer. They will come back and ask for more. They will demand their own keys and their own doors.

If you are struggling with this tension, rejoice. It means that people want to go further with you. It also means they expect more of you.

Relevance is a process, not a momentary door flinging open. Most people experience relevance gradually over time, as their lives bring them back to the same room again and again, for different reasons at different times. Institutionally, we cultivate relevance when we invite people to go further with us, deeper into the room.

That's what happened with Sangye Hawke. Sangye first came to the MAH as a visitor through the front door. She added a personal memory to a participatory exhibit, and it unlocked a slice of meaning for her. Next, she visited the historical archive to make a research inquiry about genealogy. Our archivist, Marla Novo, invited Sangye in deeper. Marla invited her to participate in local research projects. To join a committee. To become a volunteer. Sangye has become one of our most valued participants at the museum and at a historical cemetery we manage. She donates time. She donates money. She donates snacks. She got her whole family involved as volunteers. She even wrote a book of historical fiction based on research she did at the cemetery. As Sangye put it, she "transformed from a house-bound depressive to a wheelbarrow pushing, excavating cemetery preservationist."

Sangye found her voice at our museum. Now, the MAH is deeply relevant to her, not just as a place to do research, but as a place to connect with friends, make discoveries, and contribute to the community.

Everybody starts at the front door. People need a reason to walk through the door the first time, and more likely than not, it will be based on something they already expect you to offer, something that fits the keychain the world handed them. But if you can go deeper, you can go further. If you can be relevant to how people define themselves in their hearts, you can open up more doors. You can reach people who weren't societally selected into your room. You can matter more to more people.

SOME DOORS ARE INVISIBLE

I run a museum in the middle of a vibrant downtown, with a big sign and banner outside. We get good press and have thousands of local enthusiasts. But every day, many people walk through the lobby quickly and unseeing, using it as a pass-through from one part of town to another. The most common thing we hear from people passing through? "I never knew what was in here."

People to whom the museum is relevant—people who already have keys to the experiences we offer—see the MAH as an open room full of art and culture. But for outsiders, the MAH is one big question mark. Maybe worth checking out. Maybe not. It is a room with a locked door. To some, the door is intriguing. To others, dull. A few on the outside feel confident that the room holds all that they desire—if only they can find the right key to the door. But most people pass by the museum unseeing, unperturbed.

When our institutions' offerings are too opaque, or require too much effort to access, we become irrelevant. Our doors aren't just hard to access. For most people on the outside, the doors don't even exist.

Invisible doors are not just the hallmark of underground gambling parlors and exclusive nightclubs. Invisible doors are everywhere. At Balboa Park, a cultural park in San Diego boasting twenty-nine performing arts organizations, museums, and cultural attractions, a 2007 study showed that many park visitors had no idea what happened inside the buildings in the park (i.e. the art venues). They experienced the park as a park. Balboa Park was relevant to them as a place to play and socialize outdoors. The buildings were not relevant to their experience, so people filtered them out.

People can only survive in an information-dense world if they pick some things to focus on and others to tune out. Try making a list of all the businesses on a block you know well. Go out to the street with your list. What did you miss? The gymnastics center? The liquor store? The law office?

Any door will always be invisible to some. There will always be some people who pass by your place unseeing, uninterested, unable to engage. That's fine. The goal is not to open doors to everyone.

But if the people you seek to involve—the people you talk about in meetings and ardently wish for—can't see your doors, then you have a problem. It's not a problem that can be solved by opening your existing doors a little wider. You need to find a way to build new doors, based on their values, that fit their keys.

That's what Betty Reid Soskin is trying to do in the National Park Service. The oldest park ranger in the National Park Service, Betty is an interpretive ranger at the Rosie the Riveter World War II Home Front National Historical Park in Richmond, CA. Her park, like others across the country, boasts huge attendance, but the people walking in the doors are not reflective of the public beyond its gates. Urban people and people of color are underrepresented in national parks as visitors, volunteers, and employees.

Betty is African-American and proud of it. She does what she can to open doors into national parks for other people of color, both as places to visit and places to build a career. Her key is her park ranger uniform. She doesn't just wear it when she clocks in at the park. She wears it in the streets of Richmond and the East Bay. She claims the uniform of the National Park Service, not just for herself, but for other people of color too. As she puts it: "Upon being seen on the streets, in an elevator or escalator, I'm announcing a career path to children of color."

But a key only works if people can see the door. One evening, Betty was on her way home from her job when she stopped at the grocery store to pick up a few things for dinner. Another customer—a black woman, like her—asked politely if Betty worked at the prison nearby. After a moment of surprise, Betty explained no, that her uniform was that of a park ranger. And then she went home.

At the time, Betty was amused—smug even—at this momentary reminder of the limitations of others' experiences. But the anecdote grew heavy in her mind in 2015, as newspapers filled with stories of police violence against African-Americans. She encountered with distressing frequency the ugly connotations of officious uniforms in her community.

Betty thought often about her unknown friend from the grocery store. The National Park Service uniform held no meaning for her. She didn't see it as a key to history and nature. She could only map it to a room of which she was aware: that of the prison system. Rangers weren't relevant to her. Prison guards were.

We don't always choose what is relevant to us. We don't always choose what doors we see. The world chooses—in ways both beautiful and hideous, based on circumstance as much as individual will. It takes an activist like Betty to open new doors and pioneer new pathways of relevance.

DUMBING IT DOWN

If you try to make your work relevant to new people, you will be accused of dumbing down your work.

It is entirely possible to dumb down your work to its detriment. It is possible to shirk the complicated bits, smooth over inconvenient data, or ignore voices of dissent. It is possible to replace serious scholarship with superficial celebrity. It is possible to avoid hard differences and settle for glossy consensus.

That's not what most people mean when they talk about dumbing down in the context of community relevance.

When people accuse institutions of dumbing down, they are more likely complaining that you are adding too many new doors into the experience. Doors that are too loud, too glittery, too ethnic, too fun. They may say you dumb down the museum when you offer an interpretative experience around the art. That you dumb down the science when you make a game about it. That you dumb down the prayer service when you offer it in English.

These things are not dumbing down. They are opening up. Yes, it affects a room when you cut new doors into its walls. But it doesn't transform what's inside the room. It just changes who can get in. That's not to say the framing of the content won't look a little different. The curve of the doorway and the message on the doormat might shift. But it needn't distort what's inside.

Building new doors is a way of making change. That change impacts people on the inside and the outside differently. Instead of talking about "traditional" approaches and "new" ones, I find it more productive to talk about insiders and outsiders. Insiders have different perspectives than outsiders. Insiders have well-developed preferences, tastes, and opinions about what's in the room. Outsiders have rudimentary opinions about what's in the room—often based on outdated experiences or no information at all.

People inside the room are invested, connected, and acutely sensitive to change. For people inside the room, clutching their hard-won keys, every new door looks like a construction site. Every new entry path feels like it shifts the room. Insiders think the existing doors are just fine. They use them all the time. Why can't new people come in the same ways they did? Why can't those outsiders follow the protocols of the room? Why don't they respect the perfect version of the room that insiders have grown sentimental about over time?

We are all grumbly insiders about something. For me, it's wilderness areas. I like my national parks hard to access, sparsely populated, and minimal in services. My idea of a perfect vacation is lugging a 40-pound backpack through hard-to-access backcountry trails. It's an experience that requires permits, maps, physical ability, gear—a long list of barriers to entry. Few people go for it. That's part of why I love it.

Is this experience of a national park relevant to most potential park users? No. And so parks have worked mightily to make their offerings more accessible—to open up new doors into nature. The biggest, most popular national parks, like Yellowstone, are jammed with people. They are outfitted with wide, flat accessible paths. There are benches to sit on, interpretative signs to read, ice cream to eat, and trinkets to buy.

These parks drive me crazy. Not because they are doing something wrong. But because when it comes to national parks, I see myself as an insider. I've got my own key lodged in my heart. I feel protective of my idea of what a park should be. I feel entitled to it.

My insider entitlement is, of course, ridiculous. The existence of crowds and popcorn in 1% of our national parks does not limit my experience. I don't need Yellowstone; I have hundreds of remote, gorgeous mountains to climb in my life. Even the vast majority of Yellowstone is wild and open. For the people who will never engage the way I do, the populated, built-up part of Yellowstone is a necessary, useful option. It may even inspire a few folks to increase their outdoor prowess and join me off the beaten path.

It's a good thing that the national parks are working to be relevant to more people. This work helps protect wildlife and wild lands. It helps people connect to the land that sustains us. It helps establish the value of wilderness protection for everyone. National parks belong to everyone. The national parks do not solely, or even mostly, belong to me and my backpacking friends. They belong to all Americans. They belong to the millions in RVs who make the trek each summer. They are the great big public, and they deserve comfort and access.

I know all of this. And yet I walk into Yellowstone, see those paved paths, and my knee-jerk reaction is that they shouldn't be there, that they "dumb it down," that they distort the wilderness.

Who am I to say that access for people in wheelchairs is less important than my experience of the park as an entirely "natural" place? As an elite park user, I have plenty of resources at my disposal, from maps to rangers to well-maintained backcountry trails. The Yellowstone visitors, who account for a vastly larger percentage of park visitors, deserve great resources as well. I'm one of those protectionist insiders. I'm experiencing the karmic pain of the disruption of a fantasy version of the park I hold dear.

And so I look back on the thousands of people streaming by me in the Yellowstone parking lot with revulsion—as a jerk. But I also identify with them and look at them with hope and excitement. They are at the park. They didn't have to be there, but they perceived the promise of value there and they came. They drove thousands of miles, and they deserve to roll along flat paths in their wheelchairs and strollers. They deserve ice cream with their geysers. They deserve their own doors in. And that's not dumb at all.

WHOSE ROOM IS THIS?

I was a new parent, having lunch with a lesbian activist, when she told me the best-kept secret of hipster parenting in Santa Cruz: the Elks Lodge.

I knew the Elks Lodge as the weird building on the hill with an overabundance of wood paneling. The Elks, or the Benevolent and Protective Order of Elks as they are officially called, are a fraternal society of do-gooders founded in 1868. For over one hundred years, they accepted white men only. It took until the mid-1990s for women and people of color to be eligible for membership, and even then, most Elks Lodges stayed white, male, and aging.

But funny things were afoot at Lodge 824 in Santa Cruz. By 2015, the Elks Lodge had become a haven for LGBT parents of young children. I didn't get it. I thought of the Elks Lodge community as a bunch of elderly guys at the bar. Then my friend explained: it was all about the pool.

The only public pool in the city of Santa Cruz was closed in the 2008 recession for four years. During that dry spell, a few enterprising families sought another place to take a dip. They noted that the Elks Lodge had a great pool, plus cheap drinks and a barbecue. So a few of them got sponsored by existing members, swore to believe in God and fight Communism, and they were in. Over time, they became a dominant force at the Lodge, taking on leadership positions and advocating for more active community involvement. They had trouble getting all the way in the room; elder Elks stuck to traditions like weekly board meetings during the workday that made it hard for newcomers to fully participate. But still, what was once a bar for old men expanded to become a community center for young families, led by a group of lesbians who only twenty years ago would have been shunned and excluded by the Elks.

You can read this story at least two ways. Is it a story about an old room made relevant for new reasons? Or is it a story about change and cooptation of someone's sacred space?

In any situation where you are trying to make something relevant, what you are really trying to do is make it relevant to new people or more people. Unless it's a brand new endeavor, you aren't starting at zero. It's already relevant to somebody. There were already Elks. There were already opera lovers. There were already insiders.

We all have our own personal Yellowstones, the insider places we want to protect from change. Embrace your inner insider for a moment. Think of something you love just as it is. A restaurant. A fictional character. An art form. A park. Now imagine someone saying publicly, "We are going to make X relevant to new people. We're going to make some changes and open it up to new folks. We need to be more inclusive."

When you are on the inside, this doesn't sound like inclusive language. It sounds threatening. It sounds like the thing that you hold dear being adulterated for public consumption. Insiders often know the totality of an entity (or have constructed their own version of it). They have a clear story about what the entity is—and isn't. And so reaching out to someone new doesn't look additive. It looks like a shift away from what was. A dilution of services, a distortion of values. That shift means loss, not gain.

Outsiders have a different view. They can't see the change the way insiders do. For them, relevance is a brand new door, an outstretched hand. It's OK if at first only one part of an entity is relevant to someone new. The exhibition that speaks to their interests. The paved walking path around Old Faithful. The pool at the Elks Lodge. The entity wasn't relevant at all previously, so if even a slice of its offerings are now relevant, the outsider has gained something worthwhile. Outsiders don't want the room rearranged in their own image. But they do want to see reflections, expansions, and distortions of their experiences in ways that allow them to form new connections.

Anytime you look at an organization and think: "They've gone too far. They ought not to do that," it's worth asking yourself why. It's rare that an entity adds something to their programming that is so divergent, and so powerful, that it injures other aspects of the institution. It may injure your idea of that institution, but it's worth asking whether it really injures the entity itself. Is the room still intact? Is there still a place for you in it? That's what matters.

To be relevant, we need to cultivate open-hearted insiders. Insiders who are thrilled to welcome in new people. Who are delighted by new experiences. The greatest gift that insiders can give outsiders is to help them build new doors. To say, I want you here—not on my terms, but on yours. I'm excited you think there might be something of value in this room. Let me help you access it.

THE PEOPLE IN THE ROOM

Open-hearted insiders are essential to efforts to engage outsiders. The way outsiders experience our work is as much about the people in the room as the contents of the room itself.

The people in the room don't change the fundamental experience. They don't make the art hang differently. They don't make the songs rewrite themselves. But they change who is in the room to see that art and hear those songs. And that can have a huge impact on people's experience of the room—and who chooses to walk in.

Imagine a party. There's food. There's music. There's laughter. That's the room a party lives in. But the party is going to feel different if everyone in the room is wearing black tie. Or if everyone is eight years old. Or if everyone is south Indian. The existing insiders have a significant impact on how newcomers experience the room.

Professionals often ignore the role that the people in the room play in the reception of the experience. We focus on the content: the art, the story, the park. We do that because we ARE the people in the room. They look like us.

White museum professionals don't think of a museum as a "white" place, because they don't experience whiteness overtly. They think of a museum as a place for art, or history, or science. Not for whiteness. But if you walk into a museum for the first time, and everyone you see is white, and you are not white, you will notice. It may bother you, or not, but you will notice. Ah, you will think. I see that these are the kind of people in this room.

And for many on the outside, this realization can be a huge barrier to entry.

At the reopening of the Whitney Museum in 2014, First Lady Michelle Obama said: "there are so many kids in this country who look at places like museums and concert halls and other cultural centers and they think to themselves, well, that's not a place for me, for someone who looks like me, for someone who comes from my neighborhood. In fact, I guarantee you that right now, there are kids living less than a mile from here who would never in a million years dream that they would be welcome in this museum.

And growing up on the South Side of Chicago, I was one of those kids myself. So I know that feeling of not belonging in a place like this. And today, as First Lady, I know how that feeling limits the horizons of far too many of our young people."

If the First Lady—someone who has risen to incredible privilege and status in this country—can empathize with the experience of outsiders, you can too. This isn't just a matter of race. We have all experienced being an outsider. We make these judgments every time we enter a new room that is dominated by a particular type of person, especially a type with which we do not identify. We see that this is the gym for the beautiful people. That everyone at the symphony is old. That there are no other women in the lab.

When we enter these spaces, we have to decide: is this relevant to me? Do I see people like me here? Do I see myself here? And if not, is it worth the effort to make a place for myself here?

GO OUTSIDE

Most of the stories in this book are about how you can change what's on the inside of the experience you offer. How you can build more doors into it. How you can work with new participants to reshape your room to be more relevant to them.

But the most direct way to be relevant has nothing to do with what's inside your room. The most direct way is to go outside, personally and institutionally, to learn from the other rooms and people out there.

Going outside helps you empathize with the challenges of being an outsider. It helps you identify the doors that others are offering into their own experiences. If you are trying to understand how to build a door for a particular community, the best way to do it is to see what kind of doors that community willingly, joyfully walks into in other contexts. You won't learn what's relevant to them on your turf. You have to do it on theirs.

Of course, to do this, you have to find a door into their world. You can do this by asking a trusted leader in that community if you can shadow her. You can do this by finding out about opportunities to volunteer at other communities' events. Or you can just show up, as a participant-observer, and see what you can learn from the experience at hand.

One of the first things you'll learn as a participant-observer is how uncomfortable it can feel to be an outsider. Embrace this discomfort. It builds empathy. Architects talk about the idea of "threshold fear"—the discomfort people have when walking into certain kinds of buildings. Think about how it feels when you walk into a bank, a library, or a tattoo studio. Each of these has a different threshold. In each case, you are walking into a different environment, a different culture, a different room. The experience of the threshold is not strictly one of architecture; it is also impacted by what kind of people you see (security guards? people like you?) and the energy in the room. Walking through a threshold into a bustling shop feels very different than walking in as its only customer.

You may not always feel "fear" when passing through an unfamiliar door, but you likely feel some discomfort. Until you can identify whether you belong in the room, your guard is up. You may start adopting the behaviors of people in the room—consciously or unconsciously—to blend in more easily. You walk with a bit more swagger. You lower your voice. You stay on guard.

And then hopefully, someone welcomes you. You hear a favorite song over the speakers. You see someone who looks like you. You start to relax. You start to feel like there is space for you in this room.

For many insiders—especially professionals—it sounds unbelievable that people would experience threshold fear in museums or theaters, synagogues or parks. How could a person possibly feel intimidated, truly frightened, of entering a museum? How scary or confusing could it be? We can't fathom that kind of fear, and so we demean or disregard it.

Don't disregard it. Try it. Go to an institution that makes you uncomfortable—a place you would never go willingly. Go to a boxing gym. Go to an uber-hip bar. Go to a place of worship that is not your own. Find a place where you feel an urge to bolt out the door the minute you walk in.

Go there alone. See what makes sense and doesn't to you. Consider what intimidates you and what you feel comfortable with. Note the people, areas, or experiences you gravitate to as safe starting points.

If you find yourself resisting going to that bar or mosque, you're not alone. This is why so many of us stay in the swim lane of what's familiar to us. We don't seek out things that might be relevant but engender too much stress, effort, or uncertainty. If you feel that way about entering a particular community, folks in that community may feel the same way about coming to yours. The first step to being an open-hearted insider is feeling empathy for outsiders and their experiences.

INSIDE-OUTSIDERS

Inside every room, there are outsiders who have found their way in the door. They may not look like the others in the room, but they are often just as passionate about what it offers as everyone else.

Remember Betty Reid Soskin, America's oldest park ranger? Betty first got involved with the National Park Service in 2003, when she was asked to be a member of a planning committee for a new park in Richmond, CA. Richmond boasts the largest collection of intact historic buildings from World War II. During the war, it was a shipyard that cranked out victory ships. The new park would celebrate the home front effort during World War II, and significantly, the "Rosie the Riveters" who worked there.

The planning committee could have been a formality, but Betty took it seriously. The Richmond shipyards were deeply relevant to her. Betty worked there during World War II when she was in her twenties. But she was no Rosie.

As Betty informed the planning committee, kindly but clearly, Rosie the Riveter was a white woman's story. The image of a white woman putting down her apron and picking up a welding torch held little resonance for someone like Betty, who came from generations of working black women and herself worked in a segregated union hall on the Richmond home front. Worse, it whitewashed the history of Richmond, a majority-minority city to which tens of thousands of African-Americans had immigrated during World War II. Those African-Americans, like so many adults during World War II, were heroes who uprooted their families and changed their lives to help the Allies win the war. If the new park focused solely on Rosie the Riveter and white stories of the home front, Betty feared it would disenfranchise the many local African-Americans who had made extraordinary contributions to the war effort.

Betty received a formal invitation into the room of the park planning committee. Once there, she fought to be heard. She found space for herself and her passion in the room. Inspired by her participation on that planning committee, Betty went further. She became an interpretive ranger for the park when it opened, putting on her National Park Service uniform for the first time at the age of 85. Now, Betty tells her story to visitors at the park, proclaiming her and so many people of colors' membership in the effort to save the world in World War II.

Betty Reid Soskin became an inside-outsider in the National Park Service. Insiders often look to inside-outsiders to be representatives of their communities. If you're the only Asian person on the committee or the only teenager in the room, people expect you to speak up for your experience. You may be asked to be an ambassador for the room, forging new doors for more people like you.

Some inside-outsiders take on these challenges with grace and eagerness, like Betty Reid Soskin. But they're not all Bettys. Maintaining dual consciousness is confusing. Inside-outsiders are like transfer students. They are in the room. They want to be there. But they don't speak the language perfectly. Their prior experiences are different. They come from another place.

Frequently, inside-outsiders are alone. The only person of color on the board, the only conservative on the liberal staff, the only artist in the room. They may be tokenized or marginalized, intentionally or unintentionally. When inside-outsiders are alone, it's even more challenging for their voices to be heard. It's even easier to feel doubt or dislocation within the rooms they have chosen.

Even a confident leader like Betty experiences that dislocation. When Betty is lauded as a park ranger or a master interpreter, she often corrects people. She says: "I'm a truth-teller. Right now they call that an interpreter, so I guess that's what I am. But I never had formal training in it."

When I went to college, I became an inside-outsider. I was a female electrical engineering student at WPI, an engineering university. Female students made up 1% of the electrical engineering department overall.

I loved my school. I loved my (male) professors. I found friends—male and female. I loved the spirit of invention and experimentation. But I never quite got used to the feeling of being in a massive lecture hall, looking across the aisle, and seeing only men. Where was I, and where were the other women?

I was an outsider who loved my new room. But that did not mean I knew how I had gotten there or what made me different from other women. I gave tours to prospective students and their families in the electrical engineering building. All the students were male. I remember talking to groups of boys and their parents, pleading with them: "Tell your sisters. Tell your girlfriends. This is a good place for them too."

Theoretically I was a representative for women in engineering. I was even enthusiastic about being that representative to some extent. But that didn't make me an effective recruiter of female students. It wasn't my job, and moreover, I had no idea how to do it. I didn't have a chance to talk with young women—the ones who weren't coming on the tours—and share why electrical engineering was relevant to me. No one in the administration asked me how I got interested or tried to glean what had made WPI relevant to me. All I knew was that it was.

Betty Reid Soskin knew the door that she had been invited into: the park planning committee. Most inside-outsiders can't trace the exact door that let them into the room. It's not the job of inside-outsiders to figure out how they got in. It's the job of insiders to welcome them, listen to them, support them, and see what can be learned about how to make the room relevant to more outsiders.

OTHERIZING OUTSIDERS

What happens when institutions remain deaf to the needs of outsiders? In the worst cases, an outsider comes in, and an insider is completely unequipped to welcome that person on their own terms.

PhD candidate Porchia Moore experienced this firsthand. She was standing in an elegant room of an historic house museum with twenty-five other museum professionals from across her southern state on a bus tour as part of a conference. They crowded into a tiny room adorned with heavy drapery, high-backed chairs, and Civil War-era paintings above marble-topped fireplaces. And then things fell apart.

As the tour guide summed up his brief intro, he turned, pointed, and looked at Porchia, the only black person in the room. He asked her name and told her not to worry. That "in the end, it all worked out" for her and her people. In fact, to dramatize how wonderfully things worked out, he would give Porchia the opportunity to wave a flag at the end of his tour signaling the end of the war and the end of slavery. Throughout the tour, the guide peppered every other sentence with slave references while pointing or referring to Porchia. "Porchia, you are going to like this," he said as he talked about the enslaved peoples who worked in the home, including many happy, well-adjusted "mammies" that lived and worked there. As he kept asking the group to gather closer around him, Porchia began to retreat so that soon she was almost in another room.

Eventually, after another egregious exchange, one of Porchia's colleagues abruptly ended the tour. Some people were angry. Others embarrassed. A few were not sure what to make of what had happened.

What had happened? The tour guide made a genuine attempt at making the tour relevant to Porchia. But he did it on his terms, not hers. He forced her to perform his version of blackness, instead of learning how to be relevant to her experience. He didn't just tell her the door wasn't for her. He sent her running for it.

Porchia's experience is extreme. But it happened. It happens to outsiders every day. If this happened to you, would you venture into that room—or any similar one—again?

When we invite in outsiders, of any kind, we have to do it on their terms. Not ours. It's their key. It's their door. They have given us the gift of their participation, and they deserve our interest and respect. Even if that requires learning new ways of working, speaking, or connecting. We're trying to unlock new meaning with them. And we should be willing to put in the work to make that possible.

It's not about accommodation. It's about treating everyone inside the room as whole people, with the dignity we all deserve.

OUTSIDER GUIDES

The most productive way for insiders to learn more about new communities is to engage a guide. As on any good tour, the guide doesn't just give you an entry pass. They fill you in on customs and culture, secrets and stories, along the way.

For many institutions, these guides take the form of diverse board members, staff members, or community advisors.

Ultimately, if you intend to invest in long-term relevance to a particular community, recruiting trustees and staff from that community is critical. They are the people who can lead change for your institution.

But if you are just starting out and learning about new communities, a community advisory group may be a faster way to get moving. A community advisory group is a collection of guides—from the same community or different ones—who can help you learn more about what parts of your room are most compelling, which are problematic, and where and how new doors might invite people in. They may be engaged for a single focus group session, or for months or years as a cohort of guides.

Advisory groups are only as valuable as your ability to recruit them from the outside. The people who you already know, the ones who are most likely to immediately sign on as advisors—to some extent, they are already in the door. They already think what you do is relevant. While they may be connected to outsiders, they are not outsiders themselves. They may not be the guides you need.

There are two alternatives—or corollaries—to the community advisory group that I have seen work well. The first is research. You can pay someone to recruit outsiders—real outsiders—and talk with them about their experiences. Rigorous research can yield important insights about outsiders that can help you start to understand what matters most to them.

The other option is to change the role of the community advisory group. Instead of thinking of advisors strictly as people who can help you—defining the relevance of the group on your terms—find a way to make the advisory experience one that serves their needs and interests, too.

There are several models for what this can look like. Science Gallery Dublin hosts the Leonardo Group—seventy-five creative individuals who get together four times per year to provide input on programming. The Yerba Buena Center for the Arts creates "creative ecosystems"— groups of people who are invited to convene around an evocative topic, like "the future of soul," over several months of shared inquiry. At the MAH, we've built C3—a group of forty-five diverse community leaders who make a year-long commitment to build collaborations with each other, amplifying each other's projects to build a stronger and more connected community.

In all these cases, the participants are getting as much value as the institution. They are networking with people they might not ordinarily meet, supported by institutions that provide creative, fun alternatives to stale networking events and community brainstorms. At our museum, C3 is one of our most important programs. C3 members are diverse and committed. Members get involved with each other's work as advocates, donors, and partners. They volunteer at each other's events. They help each other recruit staff and solve organizational problems.

C3 builds community. It brings new partners to our programming. But most importantly, it unlocks meaning for everyone involved.

You can structure community advisory programs however you like. But you can build something special when you shift from thinking about what's in it for your organization to considering what's in it for everyone. That's how you build relevance. You build commitment. You build value—both for the people involved and for your institution's reputation as a convener in your community.

OUTSIDE INSTITUTIONS

Some institutions don't have their own rooms to come home to. Their work lives outside. They are always guests in other communities. They are always outsiders, asking to come in.

Cornerstone Theater works this way. The theater company co-creates all of its productions with people in different communities across the United States. They often create productions in cycles, bridging many communities through sequential productions with related but unaffiliated groups. In a cycle about AIDS and its impact on the Los Angeles African-American population, they co-created one play with gay black men and another with members of black churches. In each case, they were entering a different community, with different cultural codes, with the intent to work together on a project that unlocked meaning for everyone.

There's a reason angels often show up in stories as outsiders seeking refuge. Outsiders have low status. If they are invited in, they become guests of the insiders. They participate on the terms of their hosts. They thrive—or not—based on their ability to be relevant to the customs of the room.

When organizations show up as outside guests, they humble themselves. They throw off the high status of budgets and buildings. They are people, coming to create work, hoping to be of use. It changes the dynamic. It opens new doors into the work and the communities themselves.

In New York, The Laundromat Project has created a kind of hybrid guest/host model. It's a nonprofit organization providing artist residencies and art workshops in neighborhood community centers that already exist: laundromats. Founder Risë Wilson realized that laundromats have three key ingredients that make them ripe for artistic intervention. They attract diverse, local people, many of whom are lower-income. People in laundromats have downtime while waiting for their laundry to finish. And laundromats engender a sense of casual community in a neighborhood. They are the kind of "third places" that urban theorists talk about when describing the places beyond home and work that build community.

The Laundromat Project works with artists to spark creative experiences with everyday people in their everyday lives in existing neighborhood anchors. While it started with laundromats, artists now also work in hair salons, libraries, community gardens, and parks. It's all about meeting people where they are.

Over the years, The Laundromat Project artists have produced projects that transform the physical sites and uses of laundromats in co-creation with customers. In 2007 in Bedford-Stuyvesant, artist Stephanie Dinkins built a "book bench" and free book exchange outside GiGi's Laundromat, inviting people to read freely in a neighborhood where the library had recently closed down. In 2011 in Jersey City, artist Karina Aguilera Skvirsky set up an oral history booth inside Lucky Laundromat. She collected customers' stories of neighborhood gentrification and change and transformed them into a set of postcards featuring drawings, photographs, and quotes from customers. Lucky Laundromat set up a rack and distributed the postcards after the residency was over, keeping the art—and the community conversation—moving forward. In the summer of 2013 in Harlem, artist Shani Peters created the People's Laundromat Theater—an independent film festival of short artists' films playing 24/7 at the Clean Rite Center laundromat. Customers watched, commented on, and rated the films. Neighborhood enthusiasts joined the Wash + Fold Film Club to promote, plan, and participate in related art workshops and events. The festival culminated with a red carpet awards ceremony, with winners as voted on by Clean Rite customers.

Any of these projects could have worked in a traditional

art gallery or museum setting. I could imagine an incredible institution called The Laundromat Project, full of artists doing powerful socially-engaged work.

But that institution would be a place you would have to choose to go visit in your free time. It would be a building with operational costs. It would have more limited open hours and a lady at the front desk and a whole lot of things that make it very, very different from the laundromat on the corner.

By entering neighborhood establishments as guests, The Laundromat Project artists spark new connections on the block through creative projects in places that already matter. Hopefully, they already matter to the artists themselves. The Laundromat Project encourages artists to work with laundromats in their own neighborhoods, or neighborhoods in which they are deeply invested. They use their art to spark dialogue in communities already connected by place. While the artists' work is new to the laundromat environment, the artists are thoughtful guests. They demonstrate commitment to their laundromat hosts. They work with laundromat owners to plan their activities, making sure the projects can live happily onsite and, where possible, live on beyond the residencies. They build relationships that last, rooted in humility and the desire to participate.

Cornerstone Theater and The Laundromat Project both come into new communities by listening. They both spend months getting to know their host communities, building trust before building projects. To be able to do their work, they have to demonstrate relevance. If a community doesn't see the value in what they offer, they can't succeed. Their vulnerability gives them the courage to pursue relevance fully.

If a community doesn't see the value in what they offer, they can't succeed. At the deepest level, all institutions are subject to this fact. But few of us put our stakes in it the way itinerant organizations must. If you had to leave your home in the night, would your community of participants take you in?

MAKING ROOM

If you're seeking to be relevant to new communities, you can't build new doors by yourself. You have to find outsiders from those communities with whom you can collaborate. You have to build the doors together.

Don't look for just any outsiders. Look for those "almost comes"— people who might be inclined towards your content, your experience, but for whom your doors are invisible or unappealing. Urban people of color who dig nature but haven't connected with national parks. Young women crafting and tinkering who haven't considered engineering as a career. Outsiders will help guide you to potential doorways you've never imagined. They'll help you see things about the room that can and must change. You have to get their voices in the room—or at least in your head—as you start building new doors.

This is hard to do. You won't find "almost comes" on the inside or hanging out by your existing doors. If you are interested in being relevant to a community that is new to you, you likely have low familiarity and knowledge of that community's assets, needs, and interests. You may not even know many people in that community, period. And even as you start meeting them—learning about their community, stumbling into new conversations—your existing insider community is right there, loud and in your face, drowning out the new voices you are seeking in the dark.

Sometimes insiders are dedicated participants who are emotionally, even financially, invested in things the way they are. They are readers who want "serious" poetry and none of this hip hop swill. Board members who helped build the institution. Jerk backpackers like me.

Sometimes insiders are professionals who maintain their own social codes for what is and isn't acceptable. In Cleveland in 2009, Public Library Director Felton Thomas realized the library could better serve its community by serving free lunches to poor kids during the summer,

81

when school was out of session. Felton organized a partnership with the local food bank, and they started serving thousands of meals each week in the library.

But this program was met with resistance from the inside. The library union in Cleveland fought the program and refused to participate. "We're librarians, not lunch ladies!" union protesters proclaimed. For years, union librarians looked on as library managers and teen volunteers served lunch to hungry kids in their branches. When the library entered union contract negotiations in 2013, the library wrote lunch service into the librarians' new contract. It was that important and relevant a service to provide.

It might not have taken years and a contract negotiation if there had been hungry kids and parents protesting in the library. But outsiders don't do that. They don't yet know that your institution could be relevant to their lives. You have to spend time with the outsiders you seek, learning about their expectations and strengths and fears. And when you learn something that you can act on—even if that something is counter to what insiders expect—you have to be willing to change, or at least to open up a new door in a new direction.

In 2007, I got involved in local political debate about the future of our public library system in Santa Cruz. At packed public meetings, the library staff presented research suggesting a new program model, with fewer branches, that would serve more people. They shared data about who was and wasn't using the library, arguing that they could better serve our whole community, especially low-income and Latino families, with a new approach.

And then hundreds of community members in the audience, library lovers all, stood up to argue against the new recommendations.

The result was a milquetoast compromise and a missed opportunity for increasing relevance in a changing community.

These equivocations happen all the time. The people on the outside won't show up to the meetings (certainly not on their own) where you share how your new strategy will serve them. These people aren't in the room yet. But your meetings are. So you have to bring in their voices, whether physically or just in your mind, as you weigh the path forward.

It's tempting to give up. It's easier to keep listening to the voices of insiders who already love you for what you are. It's easier to stay relevant to them and shed your dreams of being relevant to more or different people.

But you can't give up. If you believe in the work of being relevant to new communities, you have to believe those people are out there. You have to elevate their voices in your head. You have to believe that their assets and needs and dreams are just as valid as those of the insiders who are already engaged.

Every time an existing patron expresses concern about a change, you have to imagine the voices in your head of those potential new patrons who will be elated and engaged by the change. You have to hear their voices loud and clear.

These voices are your lifeline to the future. I've hung on the hope of them every time I pushed aside dusty furniture to make room for change. When people questioned our commitment to bilingual exhibit labels, I imagined Latina abuelas chatting in the galleries with their families. When purists argued hands-on activities didn't belong in an art museum, I heard future crafters clicking their knitting needles. When older patrons expressed alarm about Friday night festivals, I listened for the teens who would one day take the stage. When a disgusted letter to the editor asked why we were showcasing so many "victims' stories" in our history gallery, I heard all the people whose history had been ignored getting the space due to them. When a political cartoon portrayed me as the harbinger of the apocalypse... well, that time I just laughed. I knew by then we'd made enough change to make a difference. I knew our new insiders would write angry letters to the editor and cancel their newspaper subscriptions. Our participants were making enough noise to shake things up on their own.

When you are starting to make room, these new voices don't exist yet. They are whispers from the future. But put your ear to the ground, press forward in investing in relevance, and those whispers will be roars before you know it.

RELEVANCE
AND COMMUNITY

Who should you be relevant to? Be relevant to your
community, whoever they are.

Communities are made of people with shared dreams,
interests, and backgrounds. The more you understand them,
the more easily you can unlock relevant
experiences with them.

You can build a bigger room, together.

HOW DO YOU DEFINE COMMUNITY?

Close your eyes and imagine your organization's "community." Is it a mist of good feeling? A fellowship of uncertainty? Does it have a human face?

Communities are people. They are not abstractions. They are not rhetoric. They are human beings.

You can't talk personally with each of the people in your community of interest to understand their individual wants and needs. You may have hundreds, thousands, millions of bodies and dreams and desires walking through your doors. So you have to think about people in clusters. Communities.

A community is a group of people who share something in common. You can define a community by the shared attributes of the people in it and/or by the strength of the connections among them. You need a bunch of people who are alike in some way, who feel some sense of belonging or interpersonal connection.

If you want to be able to generalize about individuals within a group, their shared attributes are most important to understand. To involve or mobilize individuals within the group, the strength of the connections is most important. Communities may be huge and diffuse, or niche and tightly connected. The key is to be specific about whom you seek.

So how do you get to a tighter definition of "community?"

One easy place to start is to make a list of the people to whom you are already relevant. Who loves you? Who's connected to you? Who are your existing insiders?

Retired blue-collar men who love to tinker with cars. Skateboarding teenagers using your plaza as a park. Moms with toddlers from the housing complex across the street. Artsy college students with weird haircuts. Capoeira dancers with their drums.

Start listing communities, and you'll notice that the shared attributes that bind them are varied. Sometimes, a community is defined by place—where people live, work, or play. Sometimes, a community is defined by identity—which may be externally assigned (like race) or internally defined (like religion). Sometimes by affinity—something people like to do and do together. Sometimes by affiliation—people you know, experiences you've shared, values you hold in common.

These shared attributes are not distinct. A community of people who go to trivia night at a neighborhood bar could identify by place (the bar), identity (nerds), affinity (trivia), or affiliation (old friends).

How much does the strength of connections among members matter to the definition of community? A strong community engenders fellowship among members, advances specific social norms, and has identifiable leaders. Weak communities are more diffuse, with members who may not even be aware of each other. These differences are useful when considering how and who to reach out to when trying to get involved with a new community. You're more likely to find a transgender community if there is an organized meet-up or support group or LGBT community center, marketed in some visible way, likely coordinated by a leader or set of leaders. But the community exists whether it is strong or weak.

If you want to be more relevant to a community you already engage, what do you already know about the people within it? Do you know how connected people feel to each other? Are there identifiable leaders or representatives you can talk with about their shared issues, goals, and dreams?

Starting with the people you already have is a good gut check on the question of how well and clearly you can define a community. Your insiders are not monolithic. They probably can't be defined exclusively by broad demographic terms like "Gen X." More likely, they are defined by ideas like "adults who like to be creative with their children," or "urban professionals seeking community in a fast-paced world," or "retirees who rarely travel but love to learn."

Communities outside your organization are equally complex. They aren't all ones, twos, or threes. When we talk about outsiders—people we don't yet engage—there's a tendency to collapse down to the most simplistic shared attributes with little regard for the intricacies alongside them. We tend jump immediately to demographics. We want to reach teens, or young adults, or the Asian-American community.

These are painfully broad descriptors. Do you want to reach young adults who are unemployed, frustrated, and struggling to get out of their parents' basements? The jetsetters building high-powered global careers? The ones who are trying to balance love and life and art and work in a brand-new city on their own?

Just as you treat your insiders as complex people in overlapping communities, think of your outsiders the same way. Try to find the outsiders who have some credible link to what you offer—people who almost come as opposed to those who will never come. "Almost comes" are inclined towards your content but can't see your door. They are foreign, but they share some values with your insiders. A passion for nature. A curiosity about history. A desire to belong. They are outsiders who can become insiders if you can build doors that speak to them.

FINDING YOUR PEOPLE

The Waukegan Public Library had a problem. By 2010, the city was over 50% Latino. But library patrons didn't come close to matching these demographics. The library had several programs they thought were relevant to Latinos—English as a second language classes, GED certification, citizenship classes—but they weren't getting the word out effectively. Their standard marketing techniques were not motivating Latinos to participate. How could they reach the Latino adults they felt confident they could serve?

Inspired by a health care model for community engagement, the library started a program called "promotores." The idea was to recruit Latinos who had direct experience with the library to promote library experiences to others in their community. The library hired Carmen Patlan, a Latina community organizer who had worked previously for one of the largest Catholic churches in the state. Carmen used her connections to build a team of promotores—library promoters—who all had a personal story to share about how the library had affected their lives.

Gloria Velez was one of the first Waukegan Public Library promotores. Gloria had immigrated to Illinois from Colombia, and she earned her GED at the library. Like a lot of immigrants, Gloria didn't initially know that libraries offered useful, free services—but once she discovered them, she was eager to share her experience with others.

Gloria and her fellow promotores went out into their own communities to talk with other Latino adults about their hopes, dreams, and fears. They heard about community needs that fit the library's offerings, like many parents' desires to expose their kids to educational enrichment. They heard about community concerns that changed the staff's approach, like many adults' fears that the library might share personal information with immigration officials. The promotores linked up

Latinos with programs at the library that were relevant to their interests, and they provided the library with feedback to improve their offerings. The result was more Latino engagement at the library, driven by the voices of the community the library wished to serve.

Promotores are a kind of inside-outsiders. They are inside the library enough to know that it offers something valuable. But their social lives exist outside the library enough that they can effectively create a new door for newcomers—and see what aspects of the door make it suspicious, unappealing, or invisible.

The most powerful way to gain access to a new community is not by creating programming or marketing campaigns you think might fit their interests. Instead, it starts with networking. You don't need a formal program like the promotores to start learning more about a new community. You just need to go outside. Meet people in your community of interest. Try to identify their leaders, both informal and formal. Get to know them and the organizations they trust. Listen to their interests and concerns. The more you understand what matters to them and what experiences they seek, the better you can assess whether and how you can connect with them.

WANTS AND NEEDS

You may have noticed that I have framed relevance strictly from the perspective of what the participant/community wants. Where they want to go. What they want to do. What they think matters.

This is intentional. It's not about you. It's not about what you think people need or want or deserve. It's about them—their values, their priorities.

In 2007, I sat on a panel at the National Academies of Science about the future of museums and libraries. I was the youngest person there, cowed by the leaders and experts in the room. I'll never forget a distinguished CEO, banging his fist on the table and saying, "Our job is not to give people what they want but what they need."

I was too nervous to say anything at the time, but the phrase stuck like a thorn in my brain stem. The thorn jammed in a little further each time I heard it, dozens of times over the years, in meetings and conferences and brainstorming sessions.

This phrase drives me nuts. It smacks of paternalism. As if it weren't enough to be the experts on our subject matter. Now we're the experts on what people "need" too?

I don't think we can tell the difference between what people want and what they need.

I know what my dog needs. He needs two cups of food per day. He wants a million cups of food per day. I think it is completely reasonable for me to give him not what he wants but what he needs.

I knew what my newborn needed. She needed to nap when she got cranky, even though she kept flailing her limbs. It was completely reasonable for me to swaddle her up and put her to bed—to give her not what she wanted but what she needed.

Very, very few people are in the "dog and baby" category. They are human beings. They are complex. I've spent a lot of time reading and engaging in visitor research, and I don't feel like I have a grasp on the difference between what people need and what they want. Does a mom want a program that includes her kids, or does she need it? Does a young artist want a performance that stimulates his work in new ways, or does he need it?

We spend a lot of time at my institution talking with people about their interests, needs, and values, but that doesn't mean that we know what an individual needs on a particular day, a particular visit. I don't know if someone needs an overview of local history or a deep dive into 1926. I don't know if they need to be empowered or provoked. I do know a bit about what they respond to, what they ignore, and what it looks like when they really tune into something. But what do they need? I assume they are just as changeable and complex as any person in that regard.

Does this mean we shouldn't care about what people want and need? Of course not. We should care deeply about these things. We should do whatever we can to discover more about peoples' desires, goals, needs, and values. But learning about someone's needs and prescribing those needs are completely different.

In my experience, the institutionally-articulated "needs" of audiences often look suspiciously like the "wants" of the profession- als speaking. Professionals want silence in the auditorium, so they say "people need respite from their busy lives." Priests want parishioners to accept the canon as presented, so they say "people need strong spiritual guidance." Teachers want students to listen attentively, so they say "kids need to learn this."

When I ask what the phrase "don't give people what they want, give them what they need" means, I am often told that we should not be pandering to people's expressed desires but presenting them with experiences that challenge them and open up new ways of seeing the world.

I agree. It is incredibly valuable for cultural institutions to present experiences that might be surprising, unexpected, or outside participants' comfort zones. But I don't typically hear this phrase deployed to argue in favor of a risky program format or an unusual piece of content. I don't hear this phrase accompanied by evidence-based articulation of "needs" of audiences. Instead, I hear this phrase used to defend traditional formats and content in the face of change. I hear "don't give people what they want, give them what I want."

Robin Dowden of the Walker Art Center once said that she knew the Walker's teen website was working because she thought it was ugly and impossible to navigate. What teenagers wanted (needed?) was a website with unicorns and sparkly text. That site was not optimized for Robin's experience as an adult. It was relevant to the teens she served, not to her.

It takes courage to embrace what different people want or need, especially when it flies in the face of insider culture or standards.

Let's not sell short the power of giving people what they want. Cultural experiences should be a pleasure. They can also be educational, challenging, empowering, political... but they must first be something people want. If we give up on the idea that people should want what we have to offer, we give up on the idea that what we have is desirable. Talking about what people need is like talking about going to the dentist. It sounds like a painful utility. I don't want to offer a service people would rather avoid. I want to offer the most desirable experience possible. I want our work to be wanted.

NEEDS AND ASSETS

Instead of nitpicking over wants and needs, I find it much more productive to explore the differences between needs and assets. I'm using "needs" to mean things people want, desire, or feel necessary, and "assets" to mean things people are proud of, have in hand, or consider strengths.

Many organizations have a service model that is strictly needs-based. The theory goes: you have needs; we have programs to address them. You're hungry; we give you food. You're illiterate; we teach you to read. You're socially isolated; we give you a community center.

While addressing needs is important, this service model can sometimes be demeaning and disempowering. It implies that the institution has all the answers. It suggests that the people served are passive consumers. It doesn't invite participants to be active agents in their own experience.

Recent research in many fields, including education, public health, and public safety, shows that we can be more effective when we focus on assets as well as needs. In asset-based programs, the institution focuses on cultivating and building on people's strengths instead of filling needs or fixing weaknesses. Instead of penalizing young bullies, asset-based crime prevention programs help assertive children take on leadership roles. Instead of lecturing families about the food pyramid, asset-based nutrition programs encourage families to share their own favorite recipes. Even when it comes to serious social challenges, evidence shows that asset-based programs can have sustained and surprising impact.

Asset-based programs especially make sense in cultural institutions, where we are often trying to invite people in on their own terms. Instead of emphasizing deficits—lack of education, culture, artistic ability— asset-based programs emphasize the cultural and creative skills that make people proud. These assets may be the languages people speak, the stories they know, the art they create.

When we tell someone that they need to spend time in nature, or when we tell local politicians that they need to fund the arts as a community priority, the arguments may come off as patronizing or out-of-touch. But if we tell someone that they can show off their adventurous side on a challenging hike, apply their technical know-how to a kinetic sculpture project, or share their cultural heritage at a community festival, we invite them to find value through assets they have or wish to develop. Building asset-based programming gives people more ownership over the end result. They have something to offer to the project as participants, not just consumers or audiences.

Assets and needs complement each other. When we address needs, we're filling essential gaps to build a solid foundation. When we strengthen assets, we're constructing skyward from that foundation.

Strong organizations know when to address needs and how to cultivate assets. When Felton Thomas came to Cleveland as its new Public Library Director in 2009, he started with a deficit-based model. His team assessed social needs in the city, looking for ways to be helpful in meeting those needs. At the time, Cleveland was struggling. The city was in a painful recession marked by high unemployment, poverty, homelessness, and food insecurity. Felton didn't just have one or two library branches in struggling neighborhoods. Almost all the branches under Felton's control were in neighborhoods hit hard by poverty.

As you may recall, one of the ways Felton identified that the library could be helpful was by providing meals to kids in the summer, when school was not in session. This needs-based program helped address a critical gap in young people's access to healthy food. At the same time, the program started to position the library as an institution relevant to the most pressing needs in the community.

Felton started looking for other ways that the library could be a relevant partner in getting the city back on its feet. Two of the basic needs Felton identified were the lack of employment for skilled professionals and the lack of job training for people who were unemployed. In this case, Felton realized that the library had a huge asset to offer: free educational services. He knew that people were eager to work, and he thought there might be an opportunity to marry the assets of the library with the assets of determined adults seeking jobs.

The Cleveland Public Library pushed forward a new initiative, the People's University. The People's University had started as an aspirational brand, a slogan that presented the library as a place for everyone to learn and better themselves. In the mid-2000s, the Cleveland Public Library started printing the motto on their doormats and websites. And then one day, Felton got a phone call from a business owner in Cleveland doing a reference check for a job applicant. "He says he graduated from the People's University," the businessman said. Felton realized that the People's University was much bigger than a brand. It was a launch point for the library to listen to patrons' dreams—what they wanted to do, where they wanted to go—and build new customized personal and workforce development programs based on those goals.

The Cleveland Public Library now hosts frequent community conversations to identify community needs and assets that the library can uniquely address. When community members asked for safer places for kids after school, the library beefed up its teen offerings and extended its food bank partnership to offer healthy snacks in the afternoon. When youth started sharing excitement about learning through technology, the library started hosting maker fairs and building maker spaces. When talented DJs and break dancers wanted to share their passion with the greater community, the library hosted Step Out Cleveland, a community-wide festival that was one part body-positive health workshops, one part getting down.

This work serves the library as much as it does the community. The library's success is built on the diversity of people who use it and value it. The library depends on the strength of the local tax base to support its operation. When Cleveland succeeds, the Cleveland Public Library succeeds. By transforming their relevance as a community resource, Felton was able to strengthen the library and the city at the same time.

COMMUNITY-FIRST PROGRAM DESIGN

So how do you create relevant work? Whether you use the language of wants or needs, strengths or assets, doing relevant work comes down to the same idea: creating projects that speak to the people you wish to engage.

At the MAH, we've gravitated towards a "community first" program planning model. It's pretty simple. Instead of designing programming and then seeking out audiences for it, we identify communities and then develop or co-create programs that are relevant to their assets, needs, and values.

Here's how we do it:

1. Define the community or communities to whom you wish to be relevant. The more specific the definition, the better.

2. Find representatives of this community—staff, volunteers, visitors, trusted partners—and learn more about their experiences. If you don't know many people in this community, this is a red flag moment. Don't assume that programs that are relevant to you or your existing audiences will be relevant to people from other backgrounds.

3. Spend more time in the community to whom you wish to be relevant. Explore their events. Meet their leaders. Get to know their dreams, points of pride, and fears. Share yours, too.

4. Develop collaborations and programs, keeping in mind what you have learned.

Let's break this down.

The first step to this "community first" process is identifying communities of interest and learning about their assets, needs, and interests.

How does this critical learning happen?

There are many ways to approach it. You can form a community advisory group. Create a focus group. Recruit new volunteers or board members. Hire new staff. Volunteer in that community. Seek out trusted leaders and make them your partners and promotores. Seek out community events and get involved.

I find that the more time my team spends in communities of interest, hiring staff from those communities, recruiting volunteers from those communities, helping out in those communities, and collaborating with leaders in those communities, the easier it is to make reasonable judgments about what is and isn't relevant. It gets easier to hear their voices in our heads when we make a decision. To imagine what they'll reject and what they'll embrace.

Then, we work with those people to identify community needs and assets. We identify needs by asking, "what are your biggest concerns about our community?" "What's missing here?" To identify assets, we ask people: "what are you most proud of?" "What do you love to do in this community?" "What do you have to offer?"

Once we've identified assets and needs, we seek out collaborators and project ideas. We don't start with the project idea and parachute in. We start with the community and build to projects.

With new communities, that can mean launching new relevant projects. In 2013, our Youth Programs Manager, Emily Hope Dobkin, was driven to find ways to support teens at the museum. She started by honing in on local teens' assets: creativity, activist energy, free time in the afternoon, and their needs: desire to make a difference, desire to be heard, desire to belong. She surveyed existing local programs. The most successful programs fostered youth leadership in various areas like agriculture, technology, and health. But there was no such program focused on the arts, despite a huge population of creative youth. The assets and needs were there, and Subjects to Change was born.

Subjects to Change is a program that puts teens in the driver's seat and gives them real responsibility and creative leadership opportunities at our museum and in collaborations across the county. The teens host events. They launch creative projects. They bring art to local activist efforts around the issues that matter most to them. They advocate for change at the MAH and throughout the community. Emily supports them, but she doesn't lead them. Subjects to Change isn't rooted in the MAH's collection, exhibitions, or existing programs. It's rooted in the assets and needs of creative teens in our county. The program works because it is teen-centered, not museum-centered.

Sometimes, we get to know a community and realize we have complementary needs and assets. Across our museum, we're making efforts to deeply engage Latino families. One of their greatest needs— as expressed by Latina moms we interviewed—is to connect their children with the cultural traditions of their homeland. So we started looking for organizations with strong assets in these areas. We honed in on the community of Oaxacan culture-bearers in the nearby Live Oak neighborhood, many of whom are connected through a grassroots organization called Senderos ("pathways" in Spanish).

Senderos puts on an incredible annual Guelaguetza festival, which brings together thousands of people for a celebration of Oaxacan food, music, and dance. Our Director of Community Engagement, Stacey Garcia, reached out to the Senderos folks who run the festival, hoping we might be able to build a partnership. Stacey went into that first meeting eager to learn how collaboration might benefit both organizations. She knew that Senderos could help us address one of our institutional needs—the desire to connect with Latino families. But what did we have to offer them?

Stacey walked out of that first meeting beaming. It turned out we had similar goals around community engagement but were approaching it from different perspectives. Each of us wanted to reach more people in our community. Senderos had an easy time reaching Latino audiences and a harder time connecting with white people. The MAH had a strong white following and weaker connections with Latinos. Senderos wanted to introduce our audience to their work just as much as we wanted to connect their audiences to our work.

We discovered—together—that each of us had assets that served the other. They had music and dance but no visual art activities; we brought free hands-on art projects to their festival. We built a partnership in which we each presented at each other's events, linking our different programming strengths and audiences. We started doing more and more together. No money changed hands. No new programs were born. It was all about us amplifying each other's assets and helping meet each other's needs.

RELEVANCE FOR ONE

If this work seems daunting on the scale of a whole community, break it down to a manageable size. Imagine a small community. A tiny one. Imagine making programming for a tiny island of just one person's assets, needs, and interests.

That's the kind of art Odyssey Works makes.

Odyssey Works is a group of artists, led by Abraham Burickson, who make immersive art experiences for one person at a time. That's right: one. For each project, Abraham and his colleagues find funding and invite prospective audience members to apply. They select their audience member and spend months getting to know that person. They spend time with them. They call references. They try to understand not just the surface of the individual's personality but the fundamental way that person sees the world, what Abraham calls their "experiencing consciousness." And then, based on their research, they remake the world for a weekend, twisting the person's environment with sensory experiences that explore and challenge their deepest inclinations.

Instead of starting with a script, this artwork starts with the audience. The audience provides an artistic challenge, a challenge like any other creative constraint. Odyssey Works starts constrained by the audience member's perspective. The audience provides an offering of their idiosyncratic way of looking at the world. They expose the keys within their hearts. The artists spend time in the rooms that matter most to the audience. They locate those familiar, favored rooms, learn what makes them meaningful, and then they start sketching new doorways out of those rooms into unexpected places.

They did that for Kristina. Kristina's Odyssey Works weekend started with something she loved: Clair de Lune by Claude Debussy. Kristina loved all things symmetrical and tonal. Throughout the day, she encountered those perfect piano notes again and again. In a classical architectural space. With her family. Each time, the music was a treat that reinforced her worldview.

Kristina started to relax. The artists who were creating this weekend for her clearly understood her world, her preferences. They weren't judging her. They understood her. She was in a space of comfort. And so she started to let down her guard, to trust, to open up.

As Kristina's reservations and judgments faded, the song started to shift. She started hearing different versions of Clair de Lune. Weird ones. Discordant ones. Seven hours and 500 miles into her weekend, she got picked up at a train station by a car. During the drive that followed, she listened to a version composed just for her: an 80-minute decon- struction of the 4-minute piece. The music was a slow deterioration. It started classical and ended sounding like people chewing on string. It was beautiful noise. It was the exact opposite of what Kristina liked, and yet by that point, she found it beautiful.

Kristina's whole experience was kind of a deconstruction of form. An unwinding of the structure that rooted her life. It went from something familiar, at the heart of what she already knew, and took her somewhere strange and new. The journey made that foreign destination relevant to her for the first time.

The experience was powerful for her. She said it pried her open. After the Odyssey Works experience, Kristina changed her life. She quit her job, broke up with her boyfriend, moved to a new town.

That wasn't Odyssey Works' goal. The goal was not that Kristina should change her life or enjoy discordant music. Nor was it about creating a moment of pleasure. The goal was to create work that was both genuinely moving for her and a compelling artistic challenge for Odyssey Works. It was a love letter from someone she'd never met. It opened a door to a new level of engagement with life. It made new things relevant.

At its core, Odyssey Works' approach is about empathy and trust. They start by learning about and valuing their audience in a serious way.

Too often, when we talk about "starting from the audience," we stay at the front door. The results are superficial connections. These people like hip hop so give them hip hop. Those people like cats so give them cats. Some people show up, they seem happy, we call it a day.

Odyssey Works goes deeper. They start at the front door, and then they pick their way through the minefield of self-presentation—the surface-level selves that we show in public every day. They gain access to the precious, vulnerable dreams we guard behind walls of personality and self-presentation. They make people feel safe in their precious rooms. And then, they invite people to open up. They fling new doors open, going to wilder and further places beyond the audience's own experience. As guides, they reduce the effort required to make the journey.

Remember, relevance isn't about what's familiar or what we already like. It's about going somewhere that brings new meaning, new positive cognitive effect, to our lived experience. That's what Odyssey Works provides.

RELEVANCE FOR EVERYONE

The cynical side of me thinks about Odyssey Works and reacts, "it can't scale." It's true. We can't make millions of personalized experiences for the millions of people walking through our doors each day.

But their approach does scale. It scales on the human level, one to one, with individuals learning about the people who matter most in their lives and then sculpting new doors for them. Any time we personalize something for someone—based on what they want to receive, not what we want to offer—this happens. This is the love letter model. It's scalable to all the people and all the connections in the world.

These human connections aren't just about love. Building relationships through personalization can be big business, too. Just ask Coca-Cola.

Coke's "Share a Coke" campaign was their most successful marketing campaign in decades, reversing a ten-year slide in sales. The campaign, which started in 2011, is simple. Instead of each bottle just featuring the Coca-Cola brand, the bottles say SHARE A COKE WITH followed by a name or symbolic title. Share a Coke with Mike. Share a Coke with Dad. Share a Coke with a Dreamer. You get the idea.

The campaign works because it's personal. There is nothing as personal as your own name. And while it may not be a love letter, seeing your name on a bottle of Coke in a drugstore can elicit the same kind of emotional jolt. It accommodates that deep desire to be seen, to be noticed, to be valued.

It also works because it's interpersonal. The idea is to share the Coke. And share people do. They buy bottles as mementos for friends of a given name. They snap photos to send to friends overseas. On holidays like Mother's Day and Veterans Day, they buy tons of bottles to honor that special someone.

Coke made a universal product personally relevant to individuals.

They made it a vehicle for building relationships. Simple. Brilliant.

There are ways for institutions to use this technique without buying the world a Coke. It just requires that we change the constraints we work from, the starting points for our work. Instead of asking: "How should we script the experience?" we could ask: "What do our visitors most desire? What's in their hearts? How could we start by getting to know them, and then build an experience based on that?"

Take the guided tour. Like a lot of people, I dread museum tours. They're often one-way dronefests. I hate the feeling of being trapped in someone else's perspective, their pace, their stories, without regard for what I care to know or learn.

But Vi Mar's tour was different. Vi is a tour guide at the Wing Luke Asian Museum in Seattle. When I visited in 2010, Vi launched her tour by getting to know our group personally. She had us all sit down and introduce ourselves to each other. There were eleven of us on the tour, all adults, mostly strangers. Vi started joking with us about our relationships and hometowns while making sure we all remembered each other's names. She made it clear from the start that we were expected to address each other by name and have fun with each other. She knitted us into a short-term community, connected through the tour together.

Whenever possible, Vi lightly personalized the tour to us. She frequently directed information towards individuals in the group based on background, gender, or occupation, which made us feel like she was customizing the experience for us. At one point, when talking about the Chinese men who had built the railroads in the Western US, she asked each man in the group how tall he is. 5'11". 6'1". 5'10". "You're all giants," she said. "The men who built the railroad were only 5'1", 5'3" max."

Vi drew us personally into the stories again and again, asking us to compare our own and our ancestors' experiences to the stories she told. She went back and forth between empathizing with us and asking us to empathize with the historic Chinese people she was describing. The result was a tour that was enjoyable in the taking and unforgettable afterwards.

Research supports Vi's approach. In a 2009 study at Hebrew University's Nature Park in Jerusalem, researchers found that even a few minutes spent learning about participants at the beginning of a tour can significantly enhance visitors' experiences.

The researchers worked with a guide who had been leading "Discovery Walk Tree Tours" for two years at the nature park. In the experiment, the guide made a simple change to how she started the tour. Before heading out, she asked the tour group: "When you think of trees, what comes to mind?" For three minutes, people shared their own starting points, or "entrance narratives." The guide asked follow-up questions about each one: "Where did you plant that tree?" "What did it smell like?" Wherever she could, the guide identified a potential link to the tour, saying something like "how high up was that tree house? Make sure to stop me when we get to the Sequoia. There's an amazing story I'd love to share about a woman who stayed in a primitive tree house 300 feet up in a Sequoia for two years..."

These pre-tour conversations lasted only three minutes. And then, as the tour progressed, the guide would point out these links and re-engage the group based on their personal entrance narratives. On average, the guide would reference three to five of the visitors' entrance narratives in an hour-long tour.

The researchers tested this approach against a control group—led by the same guide—who started their tour with a few minutes of friendly chatting, but not about trees.

The outcomes of the study were dramatic. The entrance narratives made the tours more interesting, educational, and memorable. Researchers found that during the tours that incorporated entrance narratives, people were much more engaged. They asked and answered more questions, discussed the content more often, wrote things down, squirmed less, even touched the trees more. And after the tours, the entrance narrative groups reported higher levels of enjoyment and learning when reflecting on the experience.

The tour guide didn't have to dumb down her tour—or even change its route—to make this effective. She just had to start with three minutes learning where her people were coming from, their context for trees, the stories and memories they held dear. She lightly wove their stories into hers. The relevance grew from there.

This principle doesn't only hold true on guided tours. You can elicit someone's entrance narrative anytime they walk through your doors. This is a simple two-step process. First, find a way to ask the person what brought them in. Then, find a way to affirm and build on their response. You might provide a special recommendation for something to see or do based on their interests. You might seat them in a particular area, help them take a group photo, or invite them to another event.

This sounds easy. But it's not easy to retrain yourself if you've spent years rattling off your offerings to each new person who approaches the desk. It's not easy to stop, ask, and listen before you speak.

We build relevance when we learn about people and connect with them on their terms. Many institutions do the first step but not the second. We ask, "what brings you here?" to better understand our marketing effectiveness and relevance outside our walls. But then we forget to build on their entrance narratives. We miss the opportunity to be more relevant inside our walls, too.

BUILD A DOOR OR CHANGE THE ROOM?

Once you understand your community of interest, you have a choice. You can build relevance by constructing new doors. Or you can change the programming within the room itself. Or both.

How can you decide when to build new doors, when to change the room, and when to do both?

Building new doors is a form of marketing. When you build a new door, you invite someone new into a pre-existing room. This strategy is successful when you have an existing room with a compelling experience and a credible sense that that experience will be relevant to your audience of interest. Remember the New World Symphony, the Miami orchestra that used night club marketing techniques to attract young urbanites to classical music? Or the promotores at the Waukegan Public Library sharing their offerings with Latino immigrants? They are in the door-building business. Building new doors, wider doors, or doors that are open different hours of the day works when you think you have the right programming to offer your community of interest—you just need to find them and invite them into the room in a welcoming manner.

Changing the room means changing programming. If you think the experience you have to offer will be challenging, confounding, or off-putting for your audience of interest, you can't just build them a door and hope for the best. You are going to have to change what you actually offer to make it relevant, as opposed to just changing how you market it. Think of the Subjects to Change teen program, or the free lunches at the Cleveland Public Library. These new programs fundamentally altered their institution's offerings. When communities of interest avoid your programming regardless of your marketing investments, you need to change the room. If people attend once and don't come back, it's probably a problem with the experience and not the marketing.

It's not always easy to make these distinctions in the real world. There are many times when we need to change the room but focus only on the door—or we embark on a room renovation and ignore the fact that the existing door doesn't give people a sense of what has changed inside.

Imagine two institutions in an ethnically-diverse city. Each decides to invest in providing content in English and Spanish as part of an effort to increase relevance to their communities. Institution A makes all its marketing materials bilingual, but changes nothing about the languages spoken inside its walls. Institution B recruits new Spanish-speaking staff to offer programs in both languages, but makes no changes to its monolingual marketing materials.

A is working the door. B is shifting the room. Each has made remarkable strides towards their goal, but each is limited by how far they've gone. Will Spanish-speaking outsiders walk into A expecting experiences en espanol and walk out disappointed? Will outsiders ignore B's programming entirely, not knowing it is para ellos?

The obvious answer is that you need both A and B. Many times, we find that we need both new doors and changed rooms, but we don't know how to sequence them for the greatest impact.

That's what happened at the London Science Museum as they worked to make their science shows relevant to deaf audiences. The museum's science shows are family-oriented presentations by high-energy performers, full of surprising experiments and explosions. Museum staff knew the shows appealed to diverse families, and they wanted to reach deaf families in particular. So they started with a new door and a slight shift to the room. They marketed the shows to deaf families at the door, and provided a sign language interpreter at the presentations in the room.

The new door and shifted room were a start, but they weren't enough. Only a handful of deaf families walked in the door, and what they got wasn't satisfying. The marketing and the changes to the science shows weren't working. For hearing audiences, the high energy of the presenter, combined with the visual and audial bangs of the experiments, made for an exciting show. But for deaf audiences, the experience was frustrating. The sign language interpreter was off to the side, far from the scientific action. That placement made it hard for deaf people to both see the fiery displays and follow the interpreter's information. The interpreter was not a high-enthusiasm actor like the presenter, which dampened the overall energy of the experience. And any loud audial bangs were either completely inaudible, or in some cases, distressing, for people who were deaf and hard of hearing.

The museum had made a real commitment to deaf families, and they wanted to get it right. They decided to try again. They took a step back and asked deaf families to help them. The museum recruited deaf families to come in, and they did some special pilot shows for deaf families only. Hearing staff members couldn't identify the issues that made the shows unappealing for deaf families—but deaf people could. The focus groups helped the museum understand the need for sign language performers, not just interpreters. They helped the museum consider the varied needs of their families, which often included both hearing and hearing-impaired family members. They helped the museum understand that word of mouth was the most important form of marketing in their tight-knit community, and that that community wanted more opportunities to get together socially. The families gave loads of feedback, which prompted the museum to change their approach.

The museum moved away from the idea of sign language interpretation as an amenity to layer onto individual science shows. Instead, staff created a monthly Saturday afternoon event called SIGNtific, geared specifically to deaf families but inclusive of all. At the door, SIGNtific days are not solely about science programming. They are about deaf-led community experiences with science. SIGNtific's new door is more relevant to deaf families and their expressed interests.

And then inside the room, they changed the shows. Instead of offering sign language interpretation as an add-on, SIGNtific shows flip the roles of presenter and interpreter. The presenters up front doing the experiments are deaf performers, supplemented by off-stage performers who provide voiceovers for hearing guests. While having sign language interpreters off to the side was a barrier to comprehension, voiceover interpretation causes no such problems. Hearing audience members can fully participate in the shows, watching the deaf performers onstage and listening to voiceover interpretation. Furthermore, the staff designed SIGNtific shows to ensure that audible bangs or noises are not essential to the scientific concepts conveyed. Which means the whole family—and anyone else who happens to visit the museum on SIGNtific days—can have a relevant, enjoyable experience with the science shows.

The London Science Museum didn't need to have a brilliant sense of the needs of deaf families to become relevant to them. They just had to be open to feedback and guidance from their new audience. They learned from their community of interest. They fixed what was broken. They changed the door and the room.

BUILDING A BIGGER ROOM

When I first came to the MAH, family experiences lived in one room: Family Art Day. Family Art Day was a monthly Saturday workshop. For a couple of hours, an artist would lead a project for a group of families. About twenty kids and adults would have a great time together in our little classroom. And then they would leave, staying away until the next Family Art Day.

Unsurprisingly, a whole lot of local families had no idea that Family Art Day existed. And because it was the MAH's only offering that really engaged families, most families didn't know the museum was there for them at all. As one mom said to me early in my tenure, "do they even allow kids in that museum?"

Early on, I made it a priority to welcome families into the MAH— not just for Family Art Day, but for lots of museum experiences. We added a hands-on art activity into our ongoing First Friday festivals. We started layering all-ages participatory activities into our exhibitions. And we launched a new festival series, Third Friday, that offered dozens of hands-on activities and community workshops.

None of these new activities were targeted explicitly to families, but each welcomed them to take part alongside adults without children. There were doors for families into these experiences.

As time went on, we noticed something that surprised us: families stopped coming to Family Art Day. It got to the point where we would have hundreds of mixed-age families at the MAH on a Friday night, and then only a handful the following day for Family Art Day.

What was going on here? We had opened new doors into our exhibitions and Friday night festivals, and we found that families found more value in those intergenerational rooms than the rooms (and doors) made just for them. The intergenerational rooms offered something for everyone, not just for the kids. Rather than entering a narrow door into a focused art activity in which families made their own project, people preferred wide doors into varied festival environments. They preferred rooms with a range of activities, populated by diverse people and amenities (like a bar) not found at family-only events.

So we nixed Family Art Day. That started a process for us of "de-targeting" many of our programs, shifting from offering parallel programs for separate audiences to bridged programs that connect people across differences. The result is a bigger room, one that breaks down the power imbalance between insiders and outsiders by inviting everyone in together.

I've always struggled with audience targeting. Marketers will tell you that you've got to target your message to specific communities. That if you are "for everyone," you are actually for no one... or more realistically, for whatever pack of insiders connects with your particular brand of "everyone." Better to identify your community, market to them, and then once they come inside, keep reinforcing and affirming that they are in the right place.

I understand how this works in retail—Apple people, PC people—but it seems antithetical to the public mandate that so many organizations strive to fulfill. How do you reconcile the desire to be inclusive with the practical imperative to target?

In the past, I've subscribed to the theory that an organization should target many different groups of people, offering distinct programs that connect to their different affinities, needs, and interests.

But that's still targeting. It's a way of splitting your room into many smaller rooms, some of which overlap, some of which stay separate. And while this "many rooms" approach can be effective when it comes to marketing, it's limiting if your mission is to reach and engage with a wide range of people. It leads to parallel programming: bike night for hipsters, bee night for hippies, family art day for kiddies. And rarely the twain shall meet.

At the MAH, we started addressing this challenge through a different lens: social bridging. One of our core programming goals is to build social capital by forging unexpected connections between diverse collaborators and audience members. We are eclectic matchmakers, intentionally developing events and exhibitions with unlikely partners—opera singers and ukulele players, Guggenheim fellows and amateur artists, history buffs and homeless adults. A typical project involves somewhere between ten and fifty different partners. Our goal in doing this work is to bring people together across differences and build a more connected community.

We've seen powerful results—visitors from different backgrounds getting to know each other, volunteers from different generations working together, artists from distant disciplines creating new collaborative projects. Visitors now spontaneously volunteer that "meeting new people" and "being part of a bigger community" are two of the things they love most about the MAH experience.

Our diversifying audience's interest in bridging gave us the courage to de-target audience-specific programs. This isn't just a philosophical shift—it was also driven by visitors' behavior. Families stopped showing up for Family Art Day but flocked to multi-generational cultural festivals. Teachers begged us for art and history tours instead of one or the other. Single-speaker lectures languished while lightning talks featuring teen photographers, PhD anthropologists, and street dancers were packed. Visitors eagerly walked through doors that welcomed them into rooms full of unexpected connections, eschewing doors that led to narrow, familiar experiences.

At our institution, programs that emphasize bringing diverse people together are now more popular than those that serve homogenous groups. My favorite thing to hear from long-time insiders is, "now I come to the museum and see people I wouldn't meet anywhere else." They are helping us build a bigger room.

And so, while we continue to acknowledge that specific communities have particular assets and needs, we spend more time thinking about how to connect them with each other than how to serve each on its own. We often start relationships with new communities in targeted ways, constructing doors and anterooms that speak directly to their interests and needs. But the goal is to bring everyone further into one big room, a room where we are all insiders—even if that means a jumble of eclectic furniture. We're comfortable being deliberately unhip if it means that a seven year old, a seventeen year old, and a seventy year old all feel "at home" at the museum. We like to say that the museum is like a restaurant with a big menu. Everyone should find something to their taste. But they don't have to love every item on the menu to enjoy the experience inside.

RELEVANCE
AND MISSION

Every institution has a mission that forms the structure of its room. Don't obscure it with frippery. Strip back the paint, recommit to its frame, and use it to guide you as you open new doors to new people.

STEADY IN THE STORM

When the fires hit the Okanogan Valley in the summer of 2015, everyone was affected. The forest was decimated. Residents lost their farms. Firefighters swarmed in from across the West, setting up tent cities in parking lots to fight the blaze.

Pat Verbeck's church jumped into action. She and her fellow parishioners made breakfast burritos for firefighters. They raised funds to help the community build temporary shelters for people who lost their homes. Still, one day at church, Pat found herself in a debate with a friend about whether they were being "relevant enough" to the crisis. Pat cited their good works. Her friend disagreed, saying, "we should be speaking about the fires from the pulpit, too."

What is the mission of a church? Pat's church has a mission to follow Christ by doing good deeds and helping people extract meaning from the world around them. You could argue that to be relevant in the context of the church's mission, the church had to do both things in response to the fires—good deeds and extraction of meaning from tragedy.

Pursuing an institutional mission doesn't necessarily require pursuing relevance, but the opposite is not true. Strong bids for relevance open new doors into the core of the institution—its mission.

Can an organization pursue its mission and be irrelevant to its community? Absolutely. Imagine a symphony with a mission to present the music of one composer in a particular city. If no one in that city gives a darn about that composer, you can be pitch perfect on mission and irrelevant to your community at the same time.

Can an organization pursue relevance without grounding it in its mission? Many do... at their peril. Institutions that pursue relevance without connecting it to mission run into problems of clarity and focus. They risk falsely separating their efforts to engage communities from their efforts to achieve their mission. The result is often an exhausting internal battle between "outreach" and "core" activities.

An institution's mission is its clearest statement of its purpose. If community interests are swirling around you, your mission keeps your ship steady. You don't abandon it. You use it as a rudder. It helps you know which way to turn in the storm of possibilities. It provides the confidence needed when you set out to understand your community and how you might be relevant to them.

Institutions with clouded or contested missions are like ships full of mutinous factions. Instead of one shared mission, each department has its own private version of the mission under which they operate. One department thinks the mission is about outreach. Another thinks it's about aesthetic quality. Another thinks it's about rigorous research. When an opportunity arises to be relevant to a particular community, organizational leaders go to war. If they disagree about what the mission means or how it relates to community relevance, they'll never be clear about what's worth pursuing or letting go.

Institutions with clear missions sail right past these arguments. When they know themselves and their purpose, they can honestly assess which communities are worth investing in and which bets on relevance are worth taking. They can train their eyes on the great ocean outside instead of getting stuck in the skirmishes on deck.

A HUNT FOR RELEVANCE

In 2011, the historic jet engines in the Derby Silk Mill went silent. The industrial museum, on the site of one of the first factories in the world, closed its doors.

The museum had started its life as Lombe's Mill, the first fully-mechanized factory in Northern England. Millworkers twisted silk into thread there for almost 200 years. In 1974, the site became Derby's Industrial Museum. For decades, it thrived. Visitors flocked to its collection of Rolls-Royce jet engines and artifacts reflecting the city's textile, railway and brick-making industries.

But over time, the site became a museum piece itself. Exhibitions grew stagnant and visitor numbers declined. In 2008, the Heritage Lottery Fund—a major cultural funder in the UK—denied a large grant request. The museum faced an uncertain future. In 2011, Derby City Council closed the doors and mothballed the collection.

But it wasn't closed for good. The Derby Museums Trust hired a new project manager, Hannah Fox, to reinvent what would be called the Silk Mill Museum. Hannah was given the mandate to reopen the museum again—or at least the ground floor. Implicit in this mandate was the sense that the museum had to be reinvented to be more relevant to the community.

Hannah was a museum outsider and Derby local. She knew the museum had fabulous artifacts. She'd grown up seeing those artifacts. But she didn't see those artifacts' connection to the community. The objects seemed separate from the life of the city. The museum felt exclusive and niche.

Hannah didn't just want to make the building relevant. She wanted it to be loved—and loved for the objects, stories, and history built into the walls themselves. Of course, many of the museum staff and volunteers wanted this too. But they lacked the direction on how to make the museum sing.

Instead of answering this question herself, Hannah invited community members to help via a user-centered design approach. She put aside any preconceptions of what the museum should be—including her own. There were years of reports saying it should be a museum of fashion, a museum of science and engineering, an international destination. But those were consultants telling Derby what it should be. Hannah wanted to know: what do the people of Derby want it to be?

Hannah and her team went on a hunt for relevance. They started hosting playful, public brainstorming workshops to ask locals what they really wanted to see and do. The responses were ambitious and varied. They included a cafe, a space for engineering events, science, creative activities, a concept called "Silk Mill Modern"—even for it to be used as a live music and festival venue. But across the varied perspectives, one through-line stood out: the idea of Derby as a city of makers. Derby gave the world Rolls-Royce, the Inter-City 125 High Speed Train, and the Tomb Raider computer games. One of the world's first factories was just the start of the city's story—and the right place to tell it.

Hannah tested this premise with a series of "open make" events and a mini-maker faire, co-produced with some of the locals who had participated in early brainstorming. The events were successful. They emboldened Hannah and her team to go further. They decided: we are going to remake this museum with our community. Together, we are going to make this historic factory into a place of making once more.

They turned the ground floor into a workshop, and the museum took off from there. Hundreds of volunteers showed up each week to design, prototype, and build a new experience. They designed their own personal creative projects, and they helped rebuild the museum too. They built exhibit walls. Artifact cases. Even museum furniture.

Making was the key for people to connect to the museum anew. The museum became a beloved home for makers of all stripes. Many of the museum's most enthusiastic participants were senior engineers whose career advancement had taken them away from the workbench and into desks. They felt divorced from the making that pulled them into their careers in the first place. They felt lost, tinkering in their garages, uncertain where to connect with the thing that they loved. The museum became that place.

The Silk Mill became relevant not by abandoning its core values, but by reaffirming them. Just four years after this rebirth, the Silk Mill was thriving as a museum that celebrates makers past, present, and future. User-centered design methods started to spread across the organization. In 2015, the museum embarked on a twenty-five million dollar redevelopment—funded by the same Heritage Lottery Fund that rejected its request in 2008.

The institution lost relevance when it got caught up in the stuff of the collection and the trappings of the institution. By reaching out to the community of makers in Derby, the staff learned how the museum might be valuable in a new way. Community participants helped build radical new doors into the institution, doors that reframed and reclaimed essential parts of the Silk Mill's heritage. When the museum rediscovered the makers at its heart, it found its way.

RELEVANCE IS A MOVING TARGET FOR INSTITUTIONS

Relevance is a moving target. Your content can be relevant to different people at different times for different reasons—or not. Even at institutions that have undergone radical reinvention, change doesn't stop. As Will Rogers said, "Even if you're on the right track, you'll get run over if you just sit there."

This is completely maddening. But that doesn't make it less true.

In 2008, I was invited to an unusual celebration at the Tropenmuseum in Amsterdam. The museum's director welcomed international guests—anthropologists, ethnographers, historians, designers—to celebrate the reinstallation of their whole museum. Every display and artifact had been reconfigured. But, he explained to us, we were not there to cut the ribbon and marvel at the finished product. We were there to critique the installation and to kick off its next transformation. The director said to us: "We are proud of the new installation that we share with you today. But we also know that this is day one of it becoming outdated."

Like most ethnographic museums, the Tropenmuseum's roots are complicated. It opened to the public in 1871 as a demonstration of the Netherlands' colonial riches. It was a museum of conquest and exoticism. By the 1940s, the Dutch empire had faded, and the museum morphed into a showcase of the world's cultures from a Eurocentric point of view. Every twenty years following, the Tropenmuseum changed. In the 1960s and 1970s, they addressed worldwide social issues. In the 1980s and 1990s, they embraced multi-culturalism. By the time I showed up in 2008, they had taken a post-modern approach, grappling with the roles of Dutch and other white colonialists in the cultures and stories on display.

As someone with no experience in anthropology, I was fascinated by this whirlwind tour of trends and movements in the field.

The Tropenmuseum was unapologetically working—at considerable expense—to ride the wave of relevance as societal and academic perceptions shifted over time.

On the level of an institution, this movement is admirable. The Tropenmuseum, a venerable old museum, was committed to change that would make it relevant to modern times. They recommitted again and again.

Institutions seem to approach the shifting tides of relevance in three ways: they embrace them, they fight them, or they equivocate over them.

Institutions that embrace the challenges of relevance invest in their potential. They raise the money, garner the political will, and change as needed. Sometimes the changes hit the mark, and relevance surges. The institution shines for a new day, like the Silk Mill in Derby. Sometimes they miss, and hard-working changemakers end up exhausted and disheartened.

Institutions that fight against relevance ignore its potential impact on their work—sometimes to their peril. They stay obstinately, unapologetically unchanged, hoping their dedicated insiders will keep them going until the pendulum swings back in their direction. They may even be able to attract new supporters who appreciate permanence. They might survive. Or not.

The institutions I worry most about are those that equivocate. Many institutions take a schizophrenic middle ground on relevance. They swing between issuing press releases about change while reassuring insiders that none of the good stuff will be impacted. They pat themselves on the back in the morning and go to bed fearful at night.

I don't know about you, but I want to sleep well. So I try to know myself, to know our mission, and to be honest about our intentions in the face of change.

RELEVANCE IS A MOVING TARGET FOR CONTENT

Most of us aren't steering whole institutions and mission statements. We're working on a smaller scale, with specific content or programs. But the changing tides of relevance that affect institutions affect content too—sometimes even more acutely. While an institution can pivot, presenting different content for different times, the content itself does not change. The painting is what it is.

In the nonprofit arts, administrators maintain a polite silence about the reality that certain artworks, plays, composers, and stories fall in and out of favor at different times. No museum puts up a label that says: "Our last curator thought this painting was lousy and kept it in storage. Our new curator thinks it speaks to contemporary issues and put it front and center." But we make those decisions and changes all the time. Institutionally, this is a question of moving around assets, elevating some stories and archiving others. But for the artists and objects involved, and for the people who care for them, these shifts can be dislocating. The work is the work. Sometimes it's hot, sometimes not.

I saw this when we hosted the Princes of Surf exhibition in Santa Cruz. Before the MAH exhibition, those historic surfboards rested deep in the collection storage of the Bishop Museum in Hawaii. As royal boards, they were sufficiently relevant to the Bishop's mission to be collected—but not compelling enough to warrant exhibition.

The boards were in storage for 90+ years before historians discovered they were the boards in the first known record of surfing in the Americas. The boards became rock stars in Santa Cruz. We paid a small fortune to have them conserved and shipped here for exhibition. Our community showed up in droves to honor them.

The surfboards were powerful in our community. They made magic at the MAH. But that power didn't follow them back across the ocean. After their "blockbuster" run in Santa Cruz, the boards went back in storage at the Bishop Museum, where their relevance warrants preservation but little adoration. We sent them off on the journey home with a blessing and a sigh.

The shifting relevance of these surfboards is emotional. But they're still just hunks of wood. They don't have feelings. People do.

What does it feel like to watch your own relevance ebb and flow? I grew up with a front row seat to this shape-shifting as the child of a rock musician. My dad, Scott Simon, joined the band ShaNaNa when he was 21. Forty-five years later, he's still with the band. It's the only job he's ever had.

ShaNaNa was a breakout group at the Woodstock festival, playing '50s songs at breakneck pace in gold lamé jumpsuits and grungy undershirts. They went on to build successful careers as "oldies" musicians before the term existed. They were defiantly anti-relevant in the early 1970s, a counter-countercultural throwback barreling through two-minute pop songs in the era of twenty-minute jams. At the end of every show, my dad thumbed his nose at crowds of tens of thousands, yelling: "I've got one thing to say to you f***in' hippies. ROCK AND ROLL IS HERE TO STAY." And the hippies cheered, they clapped, and they accepted ShaNaNa as part of the rollicking youth culture sweeping North America.

By the 1980s, ShaNaNa was mainstream. They were featured in the movie Grease. They hosted a TV variety show for four seasons. They became massively relevant as cultural icons, but more sanitized, less relevant to the youth culture that drives pop music. I spent school vacations in casino showrooms in Reno downing Shirley Temples while ShaNaNa entertained middle-class, middle-aged couples twice a night. In the 1970s, Bruce Springsteen opened for them. By the 1990s, their opener was an elephant.

Their audience aged with them, and they slid from hot to nostalgic. In the 2000s, ShaNaNa played state fairs. Then county fairs. Pops concerts at symphony halls. At one outdoor venue, their contract ended when the venue owners explained that ShaNaNa was attracting huge crowds of families and baby boomers... but not the 30-somethings who buy beer and generate profits. Their music was relevant to the crowd. Just not the right crowd.

Behind the scenes, ShaNaNa's relevance splintered and bubbled up in ways no one could have guessed. In the late '70s and '80s, heavy metal rockers and punks showed up at ShaNaNa's door, inspired by their early hard-driving music, anti-glam wardrobe, and street tough attitude. The Beastie Boys name-checked them as influences. They played birthday blowouts and political events and anniversary parties for long-time fans. And perhaps strangest of all, ShaNaNa's most persistent household relevance seems to be as a crossword puzzle clue (___ Na Na), fitting in a convenient box for hapless puzzle creators.

We can't fight the reality that relevance shifts over time. But we can empathize with the dislocation, the highs and lows, that comes with those shifts. Spare a thought for a humble artifact in storage. Give respect to a hardworking musician. Their power is always there to be unlocked.

YOU CAN MAKE BORING THINGS RELEVANT

When I was in my 20s, I got a professional haircut (a rarity for me). While clipping my locks, the stylist remarked, "you're so lucky. Curly hair is really 'in' right now." Her words struck me as odd. My hair has been curly from day one. It won't ever stop being curly. Why should I care if it is in or out at a given point in time?

This is the reality most of us face. We work with content that is fixed, or a mission that is fixed. And we have to figure out how to style it for different times and different trends.

But doing so doesn't have to mean buying a wig.

I started my career in science centers. I had a degree in electrical engineering, a love of math, and a desire to share that love with the rest of the world. Trouble is, most people don't see math as a hot commodity. I'm not sure math has ever had its curly hair moment.

In math and science institutions, there are two common approaches to making content relevant: connect it to daily life, or make it fun. The latter is particularly prevalent in science centers, which are full of bright colors, buttons to press, levers to pull, and explosions to enjoy. In my early career, I created puppet shows about math. Pretended to be a mad scientist doing chemistry demonstrations. Made some truly dumb jokes. The theory is that fun is always relevant to families, and thus, an easy starting point for enticing people into interest in science.

I now feel that fun is, for the most part, irrelevant to math and science. Fun is fun. It's a charming distraction. But science and math are so much more than fun. When you think about their core, the doors they can unlock—careers, invention, discovery, sense of mastery, understanding of the universe—fun is very low on the list. It's irrelevant. Like selling church services with signs about sex. Not that science isn't fun (nor that salvation isn't sexy), but it's hardly a laugh a minute.

131

Irrelevance isn't benign. It's dangerous. When we coat science and math in fun, we aren't inviting people in. We're distracting them on the doorstep.

What does it look like when we make math relevant to people on their terms?

It looks like Maths on Toast. Maths on Toast is a British nonprofit that connects families to math in new ways. Their name is based on the British truism that everything tastes better on toast: beans, marmite, cheese… and math.

Maths on Toast makes math fun. But that's not where they start. They start by acknowledging that many people think of math as boring or impossible. The way math is taught in school often feels dislocated from life, and that dislocation continues into adulthood. Most people don't spot the math they use on a daily basis. The usefulness door is invisible. The enjoyment door doesn't exist. The fun door is a fantasy.

What doors do exist? Maths on Toast starts by asking what people see as relevant when it comes to math. Despite all the negative feelings that many people have about math, everyone knows that math is necessary. They know they need to pass math tests to advance in school and get good jobs. And while math may feel like a necessary evil, the "necessary" part is key. People know they need it. Ergo, it is relevant—even if begrudgingly so.

So Maths on Toast asked families what aspect of math they felt was both needed and dreaded. The top answer: times tables. Parents and kids were spending hours trying to memorize 8 x 6 and 4 x 7. Clearly they thought it was relevant—that's why they were doing it. Trouble is, they weren't having any fun. Math felt like a room they had to slog through on their way to other goals. Could Maths on Toast make the room a little more pleasant to hang out in?

Maths on Toast staff learned more from families about the ways they love to spend time together. They learned that families enjoy spending time together making stuff, playing games, and making things up. So they decided to try to frame times tables in those terms—to make it relevant both to the desire to know math and the desire to enjoy time together as a family.

After months of testing with families in community centers and libraries, Maths on Toast developed a matching game where you have to find two cards that have the same number meaning. The 3x4 card is a match for the card that says 3+3+3+3, as well as for the card with 12 dots on it.

The game was a hit. Families enjoyed it, and children found it interesting enough to play for a long time. Part of what makes the game fun is the satisfaction of spotting a pair of cards that matches. That satisfaction is not a fancy wrapper around some boring math. The satisfaction is in the math—in making a new mathematical connection. And if you can experience that positive cognitive effect it while playing a fun game with family—even better.

Wait a second, you might be thinking. This sounds suspiciously like making math fun. How different is this times table game from the zany science workshops I facilitated at the Capital Children's Museum?

Maths on Toast established relevance based on a real understanding of their intended audiences' needs. People know that they need math to succeed, even if they dislike it. And families want to find ways to make unpleasant tasks around math (like memorizing the times table) feel like pleasant family activities. Maths on Toast started with necessary evil and ended up with interest, enjoyment, and meaning.

This is quite different from the way we approached science programming at the science centers and children's museums where I worked. In my experience, we often took an institution-centric (rather than an audience-centric) approach. We loved math. We dressed it up, splashed it around, made it loud and zany and exciting and silly. That may have been fun in the moment. It was certainly entertaining. But it may also have exacerbated the sense that math is foreign, that math is other. It certainly didn't help families unlock more enjoyable entry points into the math they were working on every day.

I don't begrudge any science center the right to make things entertaining. But even that word should give us pause. Is our goal to entertain people? Or is it to help them unlock the power of math and science in their own lives? The difference is a matter of approach, and a matter of relevance.

THE UGLIEST PAINTING ON THE BLOCK

There's a painting in my museum that many visitors hate. It's a black, shiny rectangular slab by John McCracken. McCracken was a minimalist artist famous for monolithic planks covered in monochromatic auto paint. The slabs are usually exhibited leaning up against the wall. If you were making a movie with a scene that mocks minimalist art, you'd put fake John McCracken pieces on the set.

I love talking with people about this artwork. Here are two different ways to talk with people about this piece:

1. Tell a compelling, entertaining story. McCracken believed in UFOs and aliens. He believed that he was constructing artworks that could have been created by alien life forms. Over time, his delusion deepened, and he came to believe he was creating alien portals to earth, on assignment by the aliens.

2. Ask them what they make of it. After the requisite snarky comments ("a waste of paint"), most people note their own reflection in the shiny surface. As visitors look at themselves (always a relevant and compelling experience), I tell them that McCracken was fascinated by car culture in Los Angeles—all those shiny "moving paint chips" blazing under the Southern California sun. He noticed how people would look at themselves in the shiny reflections of car exteriors, fixing their hair, pursing their lips, reinventing themselves in car windows and doors. He used automobile paint to make his bright slabs, which are like giant flat screen mirrors held up to our own narcissism. Forty years before iPhones, he imagined a future world where we are obsessed with staring into shiny black rectangles.

Both of these approaches would probably make you more interested in the work. Both stories impart a sense that artists are imaginative, that conceptual art can stem from wild ideas and connections about how the world works.

But the first story tells you about an artist who was obsessed with aliens. The big takeaway is: that guy was nuts.

The second story tells you about an artist who thought about how we relate to our own image and to screen-like devices. The big takeaway is: how do I relate to my own image?

The second approach is more relevant. It is more connected to people's daily lives, and it might be more likely to kindle a newfound interest in exploring the big questions in conceptual artworks.

Then again, given the choice, I often go with the aliens. It's too good a story to pass up.

And that's a problem. Many of us, especially those of us bubbling over with fascinating knowledge to share, prattle on about whatever we consider compelling without first questioning whether our audience cares a whit about it. We assume: the person is in the museum, ergo they want the juicy tidbits. This works as long as what we have to share is so novel that it is genuinely arresting.

But this approach is ultimately limited. Let's say you have something incredible to share. Something at the level of the aliens. Is it titillating but irrelevant? Or does it actually help someone get closer to the work? When we share shocking stories—Van Gogh's sliced ear, an affair between the ballerinas, a celebrity who recently did a photo shoot at the park—we can stimulate a strong emotional response. But we're opening a shallow door to a small section of the room. It's not clear how that initial titillation will entice someone into deeper exploration of the content and experience on offer.

Compelling information may incite a response. But that response fades quickly. It rarely yields the kind of positive cognitive effect that people can use to bring meaning to other parts of their lives.

And in reality, most of the information professionals share is neither shocking nor incredible. Most insider information is interesting at best. It doesn't make you care. It doesn't entice you to open the door. So why should you?

The urge to entertain can be a serious distraction from relevance—the kind of irrelevance that makes your work harder to access, not easier. Relevance doesn't trump compelling—it does something different. The function of relevance is to create a connection between a person and a thing, in a way that might unlock meaning for that person. If you can tell a relevant story first, you are more likely to create an appetite for other compelling information you have to share. You will unlock a deeper door. You will make meaning instead of putting on a show.

PROACTIVE RELEVANCE

I worked at the International Spy Museum in the mid-2000s, in an era of hot news stories about espionage. Bob Hanssen was convicted for selling secrets to the USSR. Valerie Plame's cover was blown. There were weekly revelations about national and international security.

Every time one of these stories hit, a reporter would call the museum. Our director would give some sound bites, maybe share some relevant artifacts, and we'd have our 15 seconds of fame. And then, nothing—until the next spy-related news broke.

This kind of relevance is passive. We waited for someone else to decide we were relevant. We responded to their requests, not the other way around.

What does it look like when an institution is actively, aggressively relevant to contemporary issues?

In 2015, a group of young classical musicians in New York wanted to take a stand on issues of race and police violence. They had watched hip hop artists write new songs sparked by the killings of black men in Ferguson and State Island. Basketball players replaced their jerseys with t-shirts reading "Hands up, don't shoot." The musicians felt called to action as well.

And so clarinetist Eun Lee, trombonist Burt Mason, and conductor James Blachly started The Dream Unfinished, an activist orchestra presenting a concert series intended to "join the chorus of calls for civil rights, social justice and an end to systemic racism." They assembled a diverse group of musicians and developed performances featuring a mix of classical music (mostly by composers of color) and speeches by leaders connected to the issues of race violence.

This wasn't a bid to co-opt the #BlackLivesMatter movement. The Dream Unfinished artists were making work as part of the movement. Their public performances helped raise funds and awareness for the issues at hand. By bridging diverse stories, musicians, and pieces of music, they helped open doors for people of color and activists to see classical music as relevant to them. They brought art to the table, claiming a space for classical music in community dialogues about race and violence. They were relevant on their community's terms by sharing the music in their hearts.

The Dream Unfinished challenged the hypocrisy they perceived in mainstream classical music institutions which invite urban people of color to buy tickets but ignore their greater community interests. As Eun Lee put it, orchestras "must address the issues that are facing the communities that they serve." Most American orchestras sit in urban centers, many of which were boiling over with racial tensions and activism in the era of #BlackLivesMatter. While many urban orchestras may have audience development programs intended to make their concerts appeal to urban people of color, few were willing to dive into the police violence issues rocking many of their hometowns.

The institutions wanted to be relevant on their own terms, not on the terms of their chosen community. Perhaps when it is politically expedient or attractive to funders or plays well to their market, those traditional orchestras will wave the flag of civil rights. But that's not what relevance requires. Relevance means waving the flag when it is needed, not when it is convenient.

CONTENT VERSUS FORM

Some institutions get caught up in chasing trends, arguing: "if people on the street are talking about X, we should be talking about X too."

No. If people on the street are talking about X, the organization should ask: is X something that matters to us, too? Does X belong in our room? And if so, how do we want to address X through the lens of our mission, content, and form?

This is not about chasing the "now." "Now" is the least useful form of relevance. "Now" is not an easy business model to chase—especially for institutions rooted in permanence. "Now" requires major changes to how we work and what we offer. "Now" comes off as disingenuous and irrelevant if done incorrectly. And now is not tomorrow. It is not the long term. It is just now. Endlessly, persistently, expensively, now.

I used to work at The Tech Museum of Innovation in San Jose, CA. Our mandate was to be the museum of Silicon Valley—not of its material history, but of its pulse of innovation. It was impossible. The exhibits we built were immediately dated. Their physicality, long development timelines, and big budgets dragged them down. They didn't dance to the thrilling drumbeat of change at the heart of Silicon Valley. They were immutable objects plunked on the sidelines.

The problem was not one of content but one of form. It wasn't that we didn't have the right stuff or stories to share. We didn't have a process, or form, to share them in the right way.

If you are grappling with relevance, changing the content you present isn't the only solution. In many situations, changing the form—process, hours, pricing, rules, techniques—is more effective. Free Shakespeare in the park makes the precious public. Flipped classrooms send lectures home and recast the classroom as a place for discussion and debate. Libraries that stay open late invite people to learn on their schedules.

Some institutions completely shift form, dramatically changing the people to whom they are relevant. When Diane Paulus wanted to connect young Boston residents to the American Repertory Theater, she turned one of their stages into a nightclub. She launched a revival of The Donkey Show, a wild retelling of Shakespeare's Midsummer's Night Dream full of salacious disco dancing, audience participation, and lots of glitter. The Donkey Show shifted the theater from a stodgy sit-down experience to a boundary-busting dance party, attracting younger, more diverse audiences to a pioneering form of experimental theater.

Any organization can experiment with new forms to open new doors. Streb Labs is a bustling urban warehouse where dancers practice, learn, and perform in a 24/7, open-access environment. The Laundromat Project presents community art workshops in laundromats. Monica Montgomery's Museum of Impact presents pop up exhibitions on human rights issues, moving quickly to collect artifacts and produce programs on the issues as they happen, where they happen.

These institutions are not being relevant by presenting cat selfies curated by a hot celebrity. They are making canonical content relevant by updating the form.

Of course, sometimes when you update form, those changes can affect the content. At Streb Labs, the open-access format of the facility makes professional dance company rehearsals public, changing the relationship between dancers, choreographers, and audiences. During open rehearsals, community members stroll through the space, sit down for a spell, take a phone call, walk out the door. Founder Elizabeth Streb and other choreographers can see in real time what makes community members tune in and out—and they often adjust the choreography accordingly to maximize audience engagement. At the Jane Addams Hull-House Museum's "Rethinking Soup" lunch series, community members share a weekly meal and discussion about social justice issues. Once the museum put that weekly lunch on the calendar, they felt committed to filling the bowl regularly with content. Sometimes, that content may be of-the-moment. Other times, grounded in the museum's collection. The weekly format doesn't prescribe contemporary content. But it makes space for it when warranted.

New formats introduce structural changes to the room, whereas new content may only change the room temporarily. Both are important, but they have different functions. Imagine a library with an author speaker series and a desire to connect with local activists. The library could make the speaker series more relevant by featuring authors speaking about politics, local issues, or civic engagement. That's changing the content. But if library's format requires booking speakers a year in advance, it's unlikely that those speakers will be able to respond to timely community issues as they arise. If the library presents the speaker series on the same evenings as city council meetings, local activists are unlikely to attend. If the library does not make room for dialogue with the audience, activists may not feel engaged.

If, on the other hand, the library shifts the format of the speaker series alongside the content, the modified program may have more relevance. If the speakers can be booked more nimbly to speak to issues of importance, if the timing fits civically-involved residents' schedules, if the audience can get involved—all of those things would likely increase the relevance of the program to local activists. Maybe the content doesn't need to change very much at all.

When an institution hosts a one-off community conversation in response to a national crisis, I often wonder: is this opportunistic? Are they taking up a hot topic briefly, making a quick change in content for this week only? I worry that they will check it off the "relevance" list and forget about it. I wonder if they will do the full work of changing formats to be more relevant in the long-term.

Format change is taxing. Changing formats means changing how you work, when your institution is open, how it's funded, and who you employ. Even a small change in format—pricing, hours, check-in process, languages spoken by staff—can require a significant effort.

The effort to change form is worth it when the alternative is constantly plugging in new content into traditional formats in a game of relevance whack-a-mole. It's expensive and tiring to keep producing one-off experiences for different audiences. One play each year for this community. One festival each year for that community. Professionals sometimes ask, "why does that community only come when we do this one program?" The answer is that that program is relevant to them. It's the only door they've got, and it's only functional once a year or once a month or however often you make that content available. When you change the form of what you do, you can build new permanent doors for new people. Doors they can use to access value anytime they want.

Want to know what it looks like when an institution uses changes in form to engage hard-to-reach audiences? That's what the next chapter is all about.

OLD PLAYS, NEW FORMS, NEW AUDIENCES

When Michelle Hensley started her theater company, she knew she wanted to do something different. Not with the content—she loved ancient Greek tragedies, Shakespeare, and modern classics—but with the audience. She didn't want to perform solely for wealthy white people. She wanted to make theater for everyone—especially people who didn't go to theater.

So she changed the form. Michelle founded a theater company that broke all the rules. Ten Thousand Things doesn't break rules for the sake of innovation. They do so to service their intention to perform for new audiences.

To reach audiences on the outside, they go outside. Ten Thousand Things primarily performs in prisons, homeless shelters, and other places for people who are struggling. Because these venues are not built for theatrical productions, Michelle kept stripping back the sets, the costumes, even the number of actors involved. She threw out the stage. These decisions started as practical choices, but they ended up charting an aesthetic course as well. They helped Michelle bring urgency and intimacy to her work. She was able to focus on the actors and not the frippery of stagecraft.

Ten Thousand Things performs complex plays with accomplished actors in a completely stripped-down format. Actors perform in full light—usually the industrial fluorescents that adorn their venues' ceilings. Actors and audience members can see each other, close up. They perform in the round, with no stage, just an area on the floor flanked with chairs on all sides. There are no sets to speak of, and little in the way of costume—just enough to create a semblance of fantasy in the very real settings of shelters and soup kitchens.

Michelle is clear: this is not theater as social work. As she puts it: "the reason I want to do theater is I want to connect with an audience, and this work allows me to do it more powerfully and clearly than anything else I do." Her company starts from the perspective of wanting to make theater for outsider audiences. They think about what their audiences will relate to, what people in the crowd will connect with. And then they make the best theater they can.

Forging relevance with outsiders is a constant push-pull between decreasing and increasing distance between the inside and the outside. On the one hand, you want to acknowledge the distance. The room is distinct. There is magic inside. The artwork has value. The room is worth entering. On the other hand, you want to draw people in, suggesting that the gulf between them and the magic is not so wide. You want to invite them to walk through the door.

Ten Thousand Things makes this push-pull work. They push by working with difficult, ancient plays. They don't simplify the texts. But the storytelling pulls their audiences in. From Michelle's perspective, ancient Greek tragedies and Shakespearian comedies are actually more relevant to struggling adults than to traditional upper-class theater audiences. The stakes in these plays are incredibly high. Characters are forced into life or death situations. They gain their freedom, lose their families, and fight for their lives. If you are in prison, or homeless, or hungry, it's relevant.

Working with ancient plays adds helpful distance to the intensity of the stories told. When Ten Thousand Things tried presenting a contemporary play in a women's shelter that told the story of a child who was removed from her mother, it felt too real. It was too painful. Women got up and left. But when they performed a fairy tale by Bertolt Brecht telling a similar story, women were able to watch that. They could explore their feelings around loss, protected by the distancing strangeness of the play's world and words.

At the same time, Ten Thousand Things removes distance in critical ways—most notably by performing without a stage, close up. The actors perform on the same surface where the audience sits, just steps away from them. They perform under bright lights, so the audience sees them and they see the audience. The cast is racially diverse, like the audiences for whom they perform. The actors are right there with the audience, flinging doors wide open.

At Ten Thousand Things performances, audience feedback is constant and unflinching. Actors and audience members look into each other's eyes and connect—or don't. People get up and walk away from performances that don't catch their interest. People lean in and cheer on their favorite characters. People get restless, or excited, and it is all there on their faces for the performers to see and learn from.

Ten Thousand Things' model has been so successful that they now offer about half the performances of each show to traditional audiences to help subsidize the work they do in nontraditional settings (where no tickets are sold). Theater insiders are often surprised at how much they love the performances. They love connecting intimately with the actors. They happily trade fancy sets and costumes for the powerful, personal experiences offered. The room that Ten Thousand Things pioneered for outsiders welcomes insiders, too. And it happened not by changing content, but by changing form.

CO-CREATING RELEVANCE

Ten Thousand Things takes an approach that is both traditional and radical. Radical, in that they are breaking down forms and conventions of how theater is produced, and for whom. Traditional, in that they present existing, canonical Western plays for audiences. Ten Thousand Things makes the plays. The audience watches.

But what about projects in which the audience co-creates the content? What about projects created in partnership with communities of interest, rooted explicitly in their voices, stories, and experiences?

There are many institutions and artists co-creating cultural experiences with community members. In the context of relevance, there are two communities worth considering. First, the co-creators. What will cause the project to unlock the most meaning for the community of co-creators involved? And second, other audiences for the finished project. What will cause the project to unlock the most meaning for outside communities—audiences for the work itself?

Let's start with the co-creators. When you work with a group to co-create a work, you build a room with them. A room filled with their stuff, their preferences, their preconceptions. But if you open that room to the public, it can shift. What started as a safe space, maybe even a hidden space, gets a garage door cut in its side. It's exciting to open that door, but it complicates its meaning.

The Foster Youth Museum is a beautiful example of this. Jamie Lee Evans started the Foster Youth Museum as a way to empower the foster youth with whom she works to tell the stories of their lives in foster care. Jamie is an activist who works at California Youth Connection, a statewide organization supporting youth as leaders in transforming the foster care system. Jamie works with transition-age youth—16-24 year-olds—who are moving out of foster care and into adult life. To say this is a challenging transition is an understatement.

36% of foster youth age out into homelessness. 70% of California prison inmates are former foster youth. Jamie, a former foster youth herself, trains these young adults to develop curriculum about foster care for child welfare professionals, becoming leaders, teachers, and advocates for change in an often devastating world.

Jamie is always looking for ways to work with these young adults from a point of relevance and deep authenticity. One day in 2005, while working with a group of "success stories"—former foster youth in their late 20s and 30s who had built strong professional careers—Jamie invited the participants to bring in personal objects that could be used to illustrate key points in their training curriculum.

The object showcase was like a show-and-tell on fire. Jamie was struck by how many adults had kept objects from foster care. These were humble objects with painful stories to tell. A woman who was frequently locked in a seclusion room in a group home had kept the sign from the seclusion room door. She ripped it from the door when she left the home. A young man who was commercially sexually exploited as a child kept the boots he had worn when he was working the streets in Hollywood. People also brought in objects of success: diplomas, law degrees, and photographs of the families they built as adults.

The group started building a vision of a Foster Youth Museum. Their first exhibition would be called the Museum of Lost Childhoods. They juxtaposed objects from people's toughest days as youth and triumphant moments as adults. The exhibition brought darkness to light. In many cases, these objects spoke to experiences their owners had never shared. Things people had locked in a deep place and never talked about.

What's the right form for something like the Foster Youth Museum? The Museum started as a precious room for the people who created it. When the Museum first started, the objects, like the stories they represented, were vulnerable. The group held mini-exhibition showings at child welfare policy summits and foster youth events. Artifacts sat on shoeboxes on folding tables. The museum was an insiders' affair. Visitors touched the objects, got close to the stories. It was humble and fierce.

Jamie and her partners in the project saw the power of the Museum as an advocacy tool. They wanted to share it with the public—and they decided the form had to evolve. They raised money. They got table-cloths. They recruited a photographer to work with them on beautiful portraits of the youth. They started treating the objects like a museum's permanent collection—a powerful idea for foster youth whose lives are marked by constant instability and frequent upheaval. They worked with a curator to elevate the display to "museum quality"—adopting the forms of more traditional exhibition design.

In 2015, they had their first big public opening, a two-week run at Grace Cathedral in San Francisco. Over 8,000 people visited the Foster Youth Museum those two weeks: foster care families, former foster youth, social workers, people of faith, civic leaders, people wandering in off the street. The exhibition was beautiful, arresting, and powerful. For foster youth and families, it was an affirmation of their lives and their value as human beings. For members of the general public, it was a wakeup call about the crises facing foster youth in California today.

Did the professionalization of the Foster Youth Museum's form make it stronger or weaken its message? Some of its early fans found the upgraded Grace Cathedral exhibition format distancing. They missed the funkiness on tabletops. But the youth involved said that elevation gave them dignity. They felt that the professional format emboldened them, protected them, and made them feel safer.

When foster youth opened up their room to the public, they needed protection. Just as the Ten Thousand Things audiences needed the distance of ancient fairy tales, foster youth needed the distance afforded by lights and professional exhibit design. Yes, that distance may have softened the rawness of some of the stories on display. But it also protected the hearts pumping at the center of the experience. The door needed a screen so there could be a door at all.

GETTING PAST THE PRETTY FISH

One of the greatest "tests" of your mission's relevance comes when you have important but controversial content to share.

For entities like the Foster Youth Museum or The Dream Unfinished, this test is easy to pass. These institutions were formed explicitly with an advocacy function. Even as they present exhibitions or classical music, they do it in the hard-hitting context of the causes they advance.

But for organizations without an explicit political function, it's tricky to present tough content. Every institution has some politics at its core—the politics of stewardship, or privacy, or care. Internally, we may pride ourselves on these values. Externally, on a few well-established battlefields, like libraries fighting against censorship, we may feel confident speaking out. But for the most part, we struggle with what to share publicly and how far to go. We struggle internally with what we believe. And we stay silent, to our detriment.

Being relevant means taking action—publicly—on the issues that matter to us and to our constituencies. Public advocacy work is good for business as well as for mission: a 2015 IMPACTS study of 48 leading US cultural institutions showed a 98% correlation between visitor perception of "delivering on mission" and financial metrics of success like fundraising ability and financial stability.

Taking public action often means taking a small piece of the room, perhaps one that happens primarily behind the scenes, and building a new doorway for it. These doors, because they are political, can be hot to the touch. But for the right communities, they unlock meaning like no others will.

The Monterey Bay Aquarium saw this firsthand when they started shifting overtly to being an advocacy organization. The Aquarium had always been a center for research and conservation work to protect endangered ocean habitats and the animals within them. But that work happened behind the fish tanks. In the front, visitors came, watched the jellyfish dance, and went home happy.

In the 1990s, the Aquarium started sharing their conservation work more directly with visitors. In 1997, they created an exhibit, Fishing for Solutions, about ocean conservation, the fishing industry, and the sustainable seafood movement. In conjunction with the exhibit, they started serving sustainable seafood in their café. Visitors started asking for a take-home version of the sustainable seafood list provided in the restaurant. Thus the Sustainable Seafood Watch campaign was born—a now-global pocket guide for people to make environmentally-responsible choices when purchasing seafood.

The Aquarium didn't stop with seafood. Inspired by their visitors' interest in advocacy, they kept building a message of positive action on behalf of the oceans across their activities. They invited visitors to write letters to Congress from the aquarium floor. They changed their mission statement to simply: "inspire conservation of the ocean." They continued to invest in conservation and advocacy work behind the scenes, and they got more and more confident sharing this work externally, through public exhibitions and programs as well as fundraising and policy change efforts.

While the Monterey Bay Aquarium is a leader in this area, they are by no means the only aquarium with a conservation focus. Almost all zoos and aquaria have conservation missions. Look at their mission statements, and you will see powerful language about working to protect animals and their habitats. Zoos spend serious money on international research projects and efforts to change the fates of animals at risk.

But here's what Monterey does that others have been reticent to do: they make their conservation mission public. Most visitors have no idea that this work is happening at zoos and aquaria. I certainly didn't—until I gave a talk at a conference for zoo and aquarium directors. Until that day, I had a vague sense of how conservation fit into zoos' educational missions, but I didn't realize the extent of the advocacy and activism happening across institutions. At that directors' conference, we talked openly about the challenge of sharing this mission with visitors. Visitors to zoos want a warm fuzzy. A family outing. Pretty fish. Do they really want to be hit over the head with gloom and doom?

This question belies a fear that the mission to conserve and protect species is not as relevant to people as the experiences on offer. On one level, this is probably true. Fewer people would come to a place called a zoo that solely presented exhibitions about the plight of the black-footed ferrets. People go to zoos to see "charismatic megafauna"—lions, tigers, and bears. It's not unusual for a zoo or aquarium to plan an exhibition and specifically slot in a certain number of especially appealing species, just as a symphony conductor might include a "crowd pleaser" in each performance.

But people do not visit zoos for cute animal antics alone. For decades, the debate about zoos' role in society has flared—and not just in academic circles. By the time I was in middle school, my friends and I had strong opinions about the ethics of zoos. Zoos were relevant to us because we had visited with our families to see the elephants and pet the goats. As our political sensibilities awoke about many issues that touch zoos—humans' role on our planet, habitat destruction, overpopulation, climate change—we wanted to apply our newfound interests to sites familiar to us, including zoos. We weren't ready to talk about what should happen on the African steppes far from our lives. But we were ready to talk about whether African elephants should be in our zoo, and whether that was a good thing, or bad.

And so we had the choice: to reject zoos or to embrace them, or somewhere in-between.

Put yourself in the shoes of a zoo director. Wouldn't you want to influence this choice? To invite those twelve-year-olds into a room where you could discuss these important issues? It seems short-sighted—both from a mission and business perspective—to abscond the opportunity to demonstrate a new layer of relevance in areas where zoos exhibit real leadership. Why not build relevance in a sphere deeply connected to your mission?

This isn't just a question for zoo directors. Many of our institutions deal directly with human controversies and political questions. Art museums deal with questions of repatriation and who should own who's cultural heritage. Theaters ask how we should dramatize the stories that matter to us. Historic sites address the battles fought and victors anointed in our collective past. Educational programs try to rebalance systemic inequities in privilege and opportunity.

With the exception of some religious and social justice institutions for whom activism is in the blood, many organizations shy away from directly addressing these big questions. They are polarizing. They are political. They could "distract" our participants from the experience they came to have.

But big issues are often the most meaningful things our institutions have to offer. They are doors to the heart of our work. To keep those doors closed is to avoid the opportunity to unlock political meaning and personal value. When we stick with the charismatic animals, we stay in the realm of the exotic, the foreign, the spectacle. When we relate those animals to issues that matter to us individually and collectively, our institutions gain relevance and value.

Sometimes our machinations to avoid the big questions damage our credibility along with our relevance. When curator Michelle Zupan chaperoned a group of high school students on a trip to the historic Isaiah Davenport House in Savannah, Georgia, the teens noticed something odd. While an exhibit panel named the slaves who worked in the 1820 home, the tour guide constantly used the word "servant" to refer to them. Finally, one of the African-American students stopped the guide and asked, "do you mean slave or were they paid?" The guide replied that they were enslaved, but that she was told not to use the word "slave" because it would offend people.

The students were very quiet and distracted for the rest of the tour. When they all sat down later, they exploded at Michelle about this "white-washed history," and wanted to know if this was how it was done everywhere. These kids were 16, 17, and 18 years old. They were ready to have an honest encounter with history. But the dishonesty of the tour cut them out of it. It destroyed the opportunity for relevance, for value, and frankly, for education in a site purportedly committed to history.

This dishonesty exists on different levels in many environments. We commit errors of omission, telling visitors a fun fact instead of something that might connect more deeply (and perhaps uncomfortably) with their lives. We write museum exhibit labels in a "neutral" tone, ignoring the multiplicity of perspectives on the issue at hand. We present the music, but we don't face the music. We say "they'll figure it out on their own."

Sometimes they will. But often they won't. The art doesn't speak for itself in every language. The archives are buried. The fish are dying far from here. If you want people to care, if you want to matter more, you have to take the risk and make the relevance explicit.

ONE CORE, MANY DOORS

There is a natural evolution of relevance for organizations in relation to their mission. Most start with one core and one door. This is both limiting and focused. A group of people start a children's museum because they want a place for their kids to learn and build community. One core: enriching children's lives. One door for families with small children seeking enrichment. If the institution successfully gets off the ground, that means the core is compelling enough to attract enough supporters and participants through the door.

As the organization grows, it seeks to expand. Inside the building, staff and board members discuss potential new programs and audiences. They start asking: how can we open more doors for more and different people to come inside?

This is the critical question. There are at least three paths institutions take in response:

1. They maintain one core, one door, and many false doors. They paint new doorways onto their exterior walls, Roadrunner-style, to attract new audiences. They hold a Dragon festival to attract Chinese families. They present a robot exhibition for older children. But they don't change the core. They don't change who the museum is really for. A few outsiders may be seduced into occasional entry, and some may find things they like inside. But many will feel tricked, confused, or unwelcome. The doors painted on for them were not sincere or didn't last.

2. They factionalize into many cores, each with its own door. There are warring ideas inside the building of what the institution is. Each faction has its own budget, its own version of the mission, and its own audience. The education team focuses on learning programs for preschool groups. The access team creates special events for families with children with special needs. The sales team pitches

birthday party packages. The single institution becomes a row of motel rooms, each serving separate clientele through separate doors. The walls are connected, but the rooms are distinct.

3. They maintain one core, and build many doors. The institution has one mission and many ways for many people to participate. This is the strongest path—and the most difficult. It takes courage and focus to maintain one core. It takes open-heartedness and humility to open many doors. It takes trust to hold it all together.

Children's Museum of Pittsburgh has one core and many doors. Director Jane Werner often describes their core as "making the North Side of Pittsburgh the best place to raise a child in the city." Of course they do this by offering great exhibitions and educational programs at their site for museum visitors. But they also invest heavily in community partnerships. They lease out parts of their building to simpatico non-profits and educational facilities. They spearhead massive campaigns to turn abandoned neighborhood buildings and parks into theaters, maker spaces, and town greens. They coordinate micro-grants for small grass-roots efforts that help youth thrive. Each of these strategies reaches different people in a different way. Each is an authentic door out into a different part of the community. But at the heart, it's all reinforcing their core focus on building a community where children of all backgrounds can succeed.

The stronger your core, the more you can reach out with confidence. The more doors you open, the more relevant you will be.

THE HEART
OF RELEVANCE

The more someone uses a key,

the more it becomes a part of them.

The room changes them, and they change the room.

PART EX-CON, PART FARMER, PART QUEEN

Each spring, Doron Comerchero walks into Pajaro Valley High School. The farmer-turned-activist is ready to sell struggling teenagers on something they may want in their hearts but don't know how to access: a ticket to a meaningful life.

Doron runs a youth development program called FoodWhat in Santa Cruz County, California. FoodWhat empowers teens to change their lives through farming and food justice.

Doron doesn't work with A students or B students. He works with kids who rarely show up to school. Kids with no food in the fridge. Kids on probation, kids struggling with addiction, kids whose lives have detoured off every map to a brighter tomorrow.

Doron believes in them. Doron supports them. And they turn their lives around.

But on day one of recruiting at Pajaro Valley High School, it is not obvious this will happen. Today, there are thirty kids fidgeting in a classroom, talking to their friends, messing with their phones. Doron's wares, on the face of it, are a tough sell. Come work in the fields, grow organic vegetables, do leadership exercises, and eat healthy food. Most of these youth have bigger issues on their minds: addiction, gang violence, social anxiety, the possibility that they may not graduate from high school or get a good job. Many of them are desperate to avoid the exhausting, low-paid farming jobs their parents hold. Why would anyone want to sign up and be part of FoodWhat?

It starts—every time—with relevance. Doron knows that if his words aren't relevant, the kids will shut him out. Shut themselves down.

So he starts at the front door, with things that are obviously relevant to them. When Doron visits schools to invite teens to apply for FoodWhat, he gives a five-minute pitch on their terms.

First, Doron throws fruit to the crowd. It wakes the kids up, builds energy, and is relevant on a basic level to anyone who is hungry. Then, he establishes credibility with stories from real kids about the program. He shows a big board of photos of FoodWhat youth at work. Farming. Cooking. Eating. Hanging out. He strategically includes images of students from Pajaro Valley High, so when he asks, "See anyone you know on here?" the likely answer is "yes." When there are FoodWhat alumni in the room, he asks them to share testimonials on the spot.

The easiest way to establish relevance—especially to something foreign—is to show that people like you, people you know, are involved. This is the front door. All you number threes—all you teenagers—this is the place for you.

Doron shows them the front door. Then he sets up the youth. He gets them to want to open the door. He answers the question on every teen's mind: "what do I get if I participate in this program?"

Doron doesn't answer this question with sweeping statements about personal transformation. He focuses on concrete things he knows are relevant to the teens in the room—especially the struggling teens who have the most to gain but are often the most reluctant to commit.

FoodWhat participants get four things. First, they get two school credits. While this may not matter to an A student, many struggling youth are miles away from the 200+ credits required to graduate. Those two credits matter to them. Second, participants get a $175 stipend if they successfully complete the program. It's not a lot, but still, money is a huge motivator for these teens. Third, graduates of the spring program get first dibs on summer internships—real jobs paying a real hourly wage. Fourth, it looks good on your resume to complete a program like this. Many of the kids in the room may not know what a resume is, but Doron explains how it helps you get a job. He explains that FoodWhat graduates get jobs all over the community—that pretty much any place you might want to work, there's probably FoodWhat alumni there. He says he will write a killer letter of recommendation for you, and when an employer is looking at two applications, that letter will move you to the top of the stack. And especially for those kids who know that their job prospects may be shaky, that sounds really good and useful.

Each of these four items is a potential key to the FoodWhat door. After offering up these four keys, Doron energizes the classroom with a challenge. He tells the kids: Don't take an application if you aren't serious. And if you are serious, make an impression on me when you turn in the application. Stand out in some way. This is a competitive program to get into, and the competition starts now.

He does all of this in five minutes. And kids come up to him, kids who were reassured that his program relates to them on the surface, kids who want to believe in themselves and have the slightest inkling this might help them do it. FoodWhat's waiting list is always a distressing mile long.

The recruitment phase is just the start of FoodWhat's relevance challenge. These are teenagers. When you talk about establishing relevance, teens are the holy grail. They are fickle. They are constantly distracted. They are self-centered. They have finely-tuned bullshit meters. They are not afraid to turn off their attention if something doesn't seem to apply to them.

Teenagers don't just need someone to help them open the door once. They need it again and again. For Doron, relevance is a process of constant reaffirmation and reconnection.

At the beginning of the FoodWhat year, it's all about getting kids to show up. If they show up at the program, they'll have a good day. Doron's team spends the first few months helping youth open the door again and again. Texting kids to remind them to come. Picking up kids when they need a ride. Reaching out to kids who seem to be fading away. If they open the door enough times, they'll figure out how to get into the room, and why it matters.

And that's just getting in the door. Once they're in the room,

Doron's team has a whole stack of techniques for going deeper with youth, helping them step into their own power on their own terms. He's managing a mansion of opportunities for relevance and meaning.

What makes teenagers such a tough crowd? Developmentally, teens are in the midst of a huge shift of agency and self-knowledge. They wrestle to assert their identities and what is relevant to them in a sea of hormonal change and uncertainty.

Before their teen years, children are sponges. They have very little agency, and as long as they are in supportive environments, they are mostly okay with that. They go where adults tell them to go. They are open to learning whatever someone else tells them is important. Relevance is not so relevant to them.

Adults, in contrast, have a lot of agency. They go where they want, choose what they want, learn what they want (within or in defiance of societal norms). Relevance is a heavy guiding hand in how adults live their lives. It is the internal voice suggesting what they might and might not want to do.

Teenagers are in the middle. They are developing self-knowledge, setting new boundaries, gaining a stronger sense of what they want and where they want to be. At the same time, their agency is still limited. They feel the friction of limited agency more acutely than their younger or older compatriots. Whenever they have some agency, they struggle to decide: is this relevant for me? Do I want to buy in? Or do I want to peel out?

In this way, teens are no different from adults who are trying something new. Think of the last time you brought something new into your life—a new activity, a lifestyle choice, a cuisine. As you sat there munching sushi for the first time, as you sweated it out in kickboxing, as you slid on that pair of skinny jeans, you probably asked yourself: is this me? Do I want this to be part of my life?

Teenagers ask themselves these questions all the time. But while most adults have a somewhat fixed sense of identity, teens' identities are in constant flux—which leads to a more complicated calculus of what is relevant, and why.

Because teens are still developing of their identities and goals, they don't just care whether something is relevant to them now. They care whether something is relevant to who they may want to be—to their idealized perception of their authentic identity. For teens, every photo they share, every activity they opt in or out of, every outfit they wear, is part of establishing their desired identity. And so even as they seek relevance, they seek relevance to a shifting target. To the person they want to be, not necessarily the person they are.

FoodWhat does this in a deep way, providing teenagers with keys to safe spaces where they can explore their potential. As one FoodWhat alumna said at the 2015 graduation: "I used to steal cars. I was going down a bad path with the wrong people. But since my time at FoodWhat, I'm living differently. Now, I have purpose. I guess you can say I'm part ex-con, part farmer, part queen."

These personal transformations start small. They start with relevance. Each week, Doron re-anchors the teens' time together on their terms. He reopens the door to the work they do together, ushering youth deeper into the opportunities before them. Each session starts with something that comes from the heart—not his heart, but the hearts of the kids in the room.

Those starters don't have to be complex. One day, the kids sit in a circle. Doron asks each teen: take a minute and think of a word that is most important to you. Then one at a time, the youth share their words and why they chose them. I'm Maria. Family is a word that matters to me. Michael. Loyalty. Jose. Happiness. Tawnesha. Trust.

Even farming tasks start with relevance. Instead of saying, "let's go weed the onions," Doron will say, "in two weeks, we want big fatty onions to put in the boxes that you take home to your parents or guardians and that we distribute out in the community." That gets them excited. They want those fatty onions for their families. They want to be proud of their work. And then Doron might layer in some science: "Onions are shallow rooters, and so are these weeds, so if we take out the weeds, we give the onions more room to get big." So now they know why they are weeding.

In a regular job, teens just get told, "do this." But by providing twenty seconds of context, the task becomes relevant. Inspiring, even. And it communicates respect to the youth involved.

Doron and his team have shaped the room of FoodWhat into a safe space for youth to step into their own power. FoodWhat's programming is relevant to the teens' struggles and dreams. This isn't superficial relevance. It's not "let's talk about celebrities" relevance. It's "open up your heart" relevance. The program invites youth to explore what matters most to them and who they want to be.

MEASURING RELEVANCE

Doron's story raises a common question about relevance: how do you measure it? If the heart of relevance is people unlocking meaning for themselves, how do you identify the moment when the key slides into the lock successfully? How do you measure something so personal and idiosyncratic? This question is especially complicated when you consider the dazzling variety of keys, doors, and rooms in action.

Answering this measurement question starts with separating relevance at the door and relevance in the room. If an institution is relevant at the door, that means people see the door and choose to walk in. If an institution is relevant inside the room, that means that people access meaning and value through the experiences the institution offers.

Here's the good news: it is completely achievable to measure relevance at the door. The easiest way to measure the effectiveness of your doors is by tracking attendance. If someone shows up, they clearly made it through the door.

If you care about being relevant to a particular community, then you have to track whether they are walking in the door. It doesn't matter if a thousand people enter if none of them are from the community to which you are trying to relate. This may require collecting demographic or psychographic data about attendees beyond the fact of their presence. Collecting this data may be awkward. Get over it. Figure it out. If you can't measure whether the people you care about are coming, you can't tell if you are moving towards greater relevance to them.

The measurement challenge starts to get trickier once people are in the room. Once people make it through the door, how can you evaluate the relevance of the experience you offer in the room? Repeat visitation is a good starting point. Presumably, if someone chooses to walk through your door more than once, they're returning because of something meaningful they found in the room. The more often

FoodWhat youth showed up at the farm, the more they demonstrated that they were finding value there.

You can also track whether people would recommend the room to others. Some institutions use the "net promoter score" in surveying, asking "on a scale of 1-10, how likely are you to recommend this service/experience/place to someone?" This question helps assess how likely the person is to hold the door open for someone else from their community to come inside. Eager ambassadors and promotores—whether formally designated or informally self-assigned—are often the greatest accelerators of new community participation.

Attendance and recommendations are useful measurements, but they don't provide much insight into the kinds or depth of meaning that people are building inside your room. Is your role in their mind fixed—as a place to learn, a place to play, a place to take mom when she is in town—or are they accessing different parts of the room at different times? What are they leaving with? If there is new meaning imparted, what will they do with it?

These questions are hard to answer via quantitative surveys at an experience. You can ask people whether they are leaving with a new idea, something they want to go deeper with, or an impulse to make a change in their own lives. But they probably won't know the answer until after they leave the room—maybe not for months afterwards. If you ask them directly, some people will lie to be nice. There's no comfortable way to check a box that says, "I got nothing out of this."

It's often more effective to identify participants' experiences through behavioral observation. If you care about whether people are accessing multiple parts of the room, you can track the diversity of activities with which participants engage. If they just come for one type of program, they're sticking to that part of the room. If they come for different things, they're navigating different parts—and the institution is likely becoming relevant to a wider set of their interests.

If you care about the depth of meaning that participants derive from the room, you can track the intensity of participants' affiliation with the institution as a proxy. When participants identify as insiders, they do so because they feel a sense of ownership and deep connection with the room. They don't just visit it; they are a part of it. And it is a part of them.

As abstract as they may seem, these feelings of affiliation are often observable. Insiders exhibit particular behaviors and take quantifiable actions. They adopt the room as their own by becoming members, volunteers, or donors. They fight to change the room—or to protect it from change—by attending public meetings, writing letters to the editor, and providing feedback when asked.

At the MAH, we've measured depth of affiliation in surveys by asking people directly about feelings of ownership and/or pride in the institution. But more importantly, we observe it in behaviors. People who call us back when we leave messages. Partners who invite us onto advisory boards for community efforts unrelated to the arts. Interns who lobby our board of directors for changes to make the institution more welcoming to them. Collaborators who spread the word about the museum to their friends and colleagues.

These behaviors are observable when they happen inside our institution. But that's not always the case. Here's where things get really tricky: often, when people unlock meaning in a room, it encourages them to take actions outside its walls. If an audience member walks out of a theater performance quietly determined to be a playwright, she doesn't keep the theater company informed about her career change. If a trip to a national park inspires a man to spend time outdoors when he gets back home, he doesn't alert the Park Service whenever he goes for a hike. If a teen in FoodWhat changes his life because of the experience, how would Doron know?

This is the hardest measurement problem. In focused programs like

FoodWhat, sometimes staff can track outcomes over time for a small number of alumni. But most organizations don't have the ability to stay in touch with participants over time. Once in a while, someone will share an anecdote about this kind of deep connection and the way it changed their life. But it's hard to systematically track the ways institutions ignite new meaning and experiences beyond their walls.

One measurable proxy for this broader impact is reputation. When an individual recommends an institution to a friend, she conveys her perception that value and meaning can be found within. When this happens on a scale of many individuals in a community—via favorable press, awards, commendations from community leaders, invitations to join boards, solicitations for endorsement—it connotes a broader reputation of value.

That said, it is important to track whether this reputation is exclusive to certain communities. If your institution has a high reputation for providing value among people who are not your target community, that's irrelevant (and possibly deleterious). If you're seen as a white institution and you want to unlock meaning for people of color, your reputation will not help you. If you're seen as a cutting-edge institution and you want to be valued by traditionalists, your reputation will not help you. If the people you care about don't care about the reputation you've built, you're unlikely to be seen as relevant or valuable to them.

How can you measure your potential relevance to people outside your room? It's less useful than you'd expect to ask them why they don't partake of your offerings. Remember, for most outsiders, the room is invisible. They don't know what's in it, and they don't know why they don't come. They just don't. So if you ask them, they'll lie. They'll say something nice, or something misleading. They'll tell you they don't come because it costs too much, when their real issue is that they believe your content is boring. They'll tell you it's too far away, when their real concern is whether they will feel welcomed there.

Outsiders are not experts about your site or the experiences you offer. They are experts about their own experiences and preferred sites—and that's the most valuable thing for you to learn more about.

Instead of asking about your institution, ask outsiders about the things they find relevant. Ask about their interests, desires, and decisions. Ask: how do you choose what to do with your free time? Where in our community do you feel most welcome and connected? What's missing in your community? What issues keep you up at night?

When you listen to their answers, you may be surprised to find connections you didn't know were there—doors that would be easy to frame out. You may also find things that challenge you—and make you question whether it is possible to build doors for those people at all.

I once participated in a workshop at the State Library of Queensland. The library was building a new center for indigenous knowledge sharing. As a public institution, they felt it was important to be a place for all kinds of knowledge in the region—not just information fit for shelves.

The library was proud—rightly so—that they had apportioned out an area inside the library to be dedicated as kuril dhagun, an indigenous knowledge center. We sat down with indigenous culture-bearers at this early meeting. We asked: how do you share knowledge? The indigenous elders told us: we pass it down in stories, told orally, from generation to generation. Fine. Check. We could have a story-sharing area, maybe even a way to capture those oral histories digitally to be shared over time.

Then the elders told us: we tell the stories with music and song. We tell the stories outside. We tell the stories around a fire.

The librarians looked around nervously. They weren't prepared to offer the kind of environment that would be truly relevant to indigenous knowledge sharing. To their credit, they identified a potential site outdoors for music, though they continued to grapple with the question of whether fire was possible or desirable. Eventually, they decided it was an essential component to add. Now, as part of kuril dhagun, the library boasts an outdoor knowledge-sharing area called the Talking Circle, complete with fire pit.

When you ask outsiders what is relevant to them, you don't just learn what matters to them. You learn what matters to you, what protocols you are able or willing to shift and which you are not. And that's a third way to measure relevance: by measuring your own institutional tolerance for relevant activities that challenge traditional ways of working. Are you willing to rebuild your room to be relevant to outsiders of interest? That's what the next chapter is all about.

TRANSFORMATIVE RELEVANCE

What happens when you discover that becoming relevant to a community of interest requires profound institutional change? At that point, you have a decision to make about your willingness to restructure your room for this community. Transformative relevance work is intense. It takes time. It requires all parties to commit. Institutional leaders have to be willing and able to reshape their traditions and practices. Community participants have to be willing to learn and change too. And everyone has to build new bridges together.

That's what happened when the Blackfoot people and the Glenbow Museum worked together over the course of twenty years to repatriate sacred medicine bundles from the museum to the Blackfoot.

This story starts in 1960s, though the story of the Blackfoot people and their dealings with museums started long before that. Blackfoot people are from four First Nations: Siksika, Kainai, Apatohsipiikani, and Ammskaapipiikani (Piikani). Together, the four nations call themselves the Niitsitapi, the Real People. The Blackfoot mostly live in what is now the province of Alberta, where the Glenbow Museum resides.

Like many ethnographic museums around the world, Glenbow holds a large number of artifacts in its collection that had belonged to native people. Many of the most holy objects in its collection were medicine bundles of the Blackfoot people.

A medicine bundle is a collection of sacred objects—mostly natural items—securely wrapped together. Traditionally, museums saw the bundles as important artifacts for researchers and the province, helping preserve and tell stories of the First Nations. Museums believed they held the bundles legally, purchased through documented sales. By protecting the bundles, museums were protecting important cultural heritage for generations to come. Many museums respected the bundles' spiritual power by not putting them on public display. They made the bundles available for native people to visit, occasionally to borrow. But not to keep.

The Blackfoot people saw it differently. For the Blackfoot, these bundles were sacred living beings, not objects. They had been passed down from the gods for use in rituals and ceremonies. Their use, and their transfer among families, was an essential part of community life and connection with the gods. The bundles were not objects that could be owned. They were sacred beings held in trust by different keepers over time. If they had been sold to museums, those sales were not spiritually valid. The bundles were not for sale or purchase by any human or institution.

Why had they been sold in the first place? Many medicine bundles had been sold to museums in the mid-1900s, when Blackfoot ceremonial practices were dying out. The 1960s were a low point in Blackfoot ceremonial participation. Ceremonial practices had ceased to be relevant to most Blackfoot people, due in large part to a century-long campaign by the Canadian government to "reeducate" native people out of their traditions. Blackfoot people are as subject to societally-conferred notions of value as anyone else. In the 1960s, when Blackfoot culture was dying, some bundle keepers may have seen the bundles as more relevant as sources of money for food than as sacred beings. Others may have sold their bundles to museums hoping the museums would keep them through dark days, holding them safe until Blackfoot culture thrived again.

By the late 1970s, that time had come. Blackfoot people were eager to reclaim their culture. They were ready to use and share the bundles once more. Museums were not. Throughout the 1970s and 1980s, Blackfoot leaders attempted to repatriate medicine bundles back to their communities from various museums. Some tried to negotiate. Others tried to take bundles by force. In all cases, they ran into walls. While some museum professionals sympathized with the desires of the Blackfoot, they did not feel that those desires outweighed the legal authority and common good argument for keeping the sacred bundles. Museums held a firm line that they were preserving these objects for all humanity, which outweighed the claim of any particular group.

In 1988, the Glenbow Museum wandered into the fray. They mounted an exhibition, The Spirit Sings: Artistic Traditions of Canada's First Peoples, that sparked native public protests. The exhibition included a sacred Mohawk mask that Mohawk representatives requested be removed from display because of its spiritual significance. More broadly, native people criticized the exhibition for presenting their culture without consulting them or inviting them into the process. The museum had broken the cardinal rule of self-determination: nothing about us, without us.

A year later, a new CEO, Bob Janes, came to Glenbow. Bob led a strategic planning process that articulated a deepened commitment to native people as key players in the development of projects related to their history and material culture. In 1990, Bob hired a new curator of ethnology, Gerry Conaty. That same year, Glenbow made its first loan of a medicine bundle—the Thunder Medicine Pipe Bundle—to the Blackfoot people.

The loan worked like this: the Weasel Moccasin family kept the Thunder Medicine Pipe Bundle for four months to use during ceremonies. Then, they returned the bundle to the museum for four months. This cycle was to continue as long as both parties agreed. This was a loan, not a transfer of ownership. There was no formal protocol behind it. It was the beginning of an experiment. It was the beginning of building relationships of mutual trust and respect.

In the 1990s, curator Gerry Conaty spent a great deal of time with Blackfoot people, in their communities. He was humbled and honored to participate as a guest in Blackfoot spiritual ceremonies. The more Gerry got to know leaders in the Blackfoot community, people like

Daniel Weasel Moccasin and Jerry Potts and Allan Pard, the more he learned about the role of medicine bundles and other sacred objects in the Blackfoot community.

And that's when things started to get uncomfortable. Gerry started to experience cognitive dissonance and a kind of dual consciousness of the bundles. As a curator, he was overwhelmed and uncomfortable when he saw people dancing with the bundles, using them in ways that his training taught him might damage them. But as a guest of the Blackfoot, he saw the bundles come alive during these ceremonies. He saw people welcome them home like long-lost relatives. He started to see the bundles differently. The Blackfoot reality of the bundles as living sacred beings began to enter his reality.

Over time, Gerry and Bob became convinced that full repatriation—not loans—was the right path forward. The bundles had sacred lives that could not be contained. They belonged with the Blackfoot people.

But the conviction to change was just the beginning of the repatriation process. The museum had to change long-held perceptions of what the bundles were, who they belonged to, and how and why they should be used. This was a broad institutional learning effort in building cultural competency. During the 1990s, Glenbow started engaging Blackfoot people as advisors on projects. Gerry hired Blackfoot people wherever he could as full participants on the curatorial team. Bob, Gerry, and Glenbow staff spent time in Blackfoot communities, learning what was important and relevant to them.

As Blackfoot elders sought to repatriate their bundles from museums, they also had to negotiate amongst themselves to re-establish the relevance and value of the bundles. They were relearning their own ceremonial rituals and the role of medicine bundles within them. They had to develop protocols for how they would adopt, revive, and recirculate the bundles within the community. Even core principles like the communal ownership of the bundles had to be reestablished. This process took just as much reshaping for Blackfoot communities as it did for the museum.

To complicate things further, the artifacts were actually the property of the province of Alberta, not Glenbow. The museum couldn't repatriate the bundles without government signoff. For years they fought to get government approval. For years, the government resisted. Government officials suggested that the Blackfoot people make replicas of the bundles, so the originals could remain "safe" at the museum. The museum and their Blackfoot partners said no. As Piikani leader Jerry Potts put it: "Well, who is alive now who can put the right spirit into new bundles and make them the way they are supposed to be? Who is there alive who can do that? Some of these bundles are thousands of years old, and they go right back to the story of Creation when Thunder gave us the ceremony. Who is around who can sit there and say they can do that?"

The museum and Blackfoot leaders had to negotiate multiple realities. They had to negotiate on the province's terms through legal battles and written contracts. They had to negotiate with museum staff about policies around collections ownership and management. They had to negotiate with native families about the use and transfer of the bundles in the community. In each arena, different approaches and styles were required. The people in the middle had to navigate them all.

But they kept building momentum through shared learning and loan projects. By 1998, the Siksika, Kainai, and Piikani had more than thirty sacred objects on loan from the Glenbow Museum. They were still fighting for the province to grant the possibility of full repatriation. Still, even as loans, some bundles had been ceremonially transferred several times throughout native communities, spreading knowledge and extending relationships. Glenbow staff had learned the importance of the bundles to entire communities. Native people were using, protecting, and sharing the bundles. Even the Glenbow board bought in. The museum had become relevant to the native people on their terms. The native people had become relevant to the museum staff on theirs. They were more than relevant; they were connected, working together on a project of shared passion and commitment.

In 1999, they put their shared commitment to the test. It became clear that they were not going to succeed at convincing the provincial cultural officials of the value of full repatriation. CEO Bob Janes went to the Glenbow Board of Trustees and told them about the stalemate. A board member brokered a meeting with the premier of Alberta so that the museum could make the case for repatriation directly. It was risky; they were flagrantly ignoring the chain of provincial command. But the gamble worked. In 2000, the First Nations Sacred Ceremonial Objects Repatriation Act was passed in the province of Alberta. The bundles went home.

At its heart, the story of the Blackfoot repatriation is the story of two communities—that of the Blackfoot people and that of the Glenbow Museum—becoming deeply relevant to each other. When relevance goes deep, it doesn't look like relevance anymore. It looks like work. It looks like friendships. It looks like shared meaning. As the museum staff understood more about what mattered to their Blackfoot partners, it came to matter to them too. Leonard Bastien, then chief of the Piikani First Nation, put it this way: "Because all things possess a soul and can, therefore, communicate with your soul, I am inclined to believe that the souls of the many sacred articles and bundles within the Glenbow Museum touched Robert Janes and Gerry Conaty in a special way, whether they knew it or not. They have been changed in profound ways through their interactions with the Blood and Peigan people and their attendance at ceremonies."

That is the power of transformative relevance.

EMPATHETIC EVANGELISTS

At its heart, building relevance is about living in the creative tension between evangelizing for the things you care about and listening with interest to what others care about. It's about radiating the inside out, and inviting the outside in.

No one does this better than religious organizations. While art institutions and government agencies are squeamish about evangelism, religious institutions embrace both evangelism and empathy whole-heartedly. Their goal is to connect people to something beyond them that also happens to live deep inside them. They wave the key aloft, sing its praises, and then they tell people: "The key is inside you. You will find your own key." It's the fundamental quest for relevance.

That's the quest Rabbi Noa Kushner is on. The rabbi has made it her mission to help people find new doors to Judaism. Noa runs The Kitchen, an un-orthodox yet serious Jewish community in San Francisco.

Jewish practice has been traditionally defined as accessible to some based on birth or conversion and not so relevant to others. It's like God was having people count off, and the Jews were all number threes. The trouble is, many American Jews—especially Gen X and younger—find that number to be completely irrelevant to the way they lead their lives. Non-Jews who might find value in Judaism feel excluded, because they weren't born into it or are not ready to convert. People think getting involved requires going all the way to conversion, which is an incredible amount of effort. It's the perfect recipe for irrelevance.

Rabbi Noa is fighting irrelevance by presenting Judaism as something you do, not something you are. From Rabbi Noa's perspective, the traditional emphasis on identity over action makes Judaism sound impossibly effortful. As she put it: "if yoga studios asked people to become yogis as a condition for taking classes, those studios would lose much of their popularity. But yoga is marketed as something one can just do; it doesn't necessitate an identity shift. As a result, people feel comfortable trying it out. Of course, once they try it, some continue in their yoga practice and it becomes a part of their lives. The same operative principle is true for us — if we want people to grow Jewishly, we need to encourage them to do Jewish first."

At the Kitchen, they don't care if you are Jewish by birth. They care if you do Jewish—if you incorporate Jewish practices into your life. The Kitchen's mission is to help people access the transformative power of Jewish religious practice. That's not about blood. It's about action.

Rabbi Noa started The Kitchen by doing informal one-on-one research with disaffected and disinterested young, urban Jews. She spent time with "almost-comes"—people who identified with some of the principles that are central to Judaism, but who didn't identify actively as Jewish. Judaism is steeped in social justice, community ritual, slowing down, personal connections—all things that mattered to the busy, young urban Jews Rabbi Noa was meeting. She learned what they valued and how they wanted to connect. She unraveled the conventions that made Judaism remote and unappealing. And then she started retying the knots, building The Kitchen to be relevant to them.

Like many of the organizations profiled in this book, the Kitchen blends clarity of purpose with eager outreach to new communities. The Kitchen is unapologetically religious ("totally religious" in their words). They practice prayer. They celebrate Jewish holidays. They run a youth program and educational seminars and community events. They pray in Hebrew. They do Jewish.

But they do Jewish in the most welcoming, inclusive ways possible. The Kitchen's programs specifically reach out to non-practicing young and middle-aged adults in form, content, and style. They built a strong, visible brand: urban, a bit sassy, and focused on building community.

And they are successful. Their services are packed. They reach Jews who haven't seen the inside of a synagogue for decades. They reach spouses and friends who never felt welcome in a Jewish space before. About 40% of their members are not Jewish by birth. And those members are enthusiastically, whole-heartedly walking in the door to Judaism, singing its praise.

Those of us working to make our work relevant are all motivated by the same evangelical impulse that drives Rabbi Noa. We believe in the power of what we offer. We believe in its potential to unlock meaning and value for people. We believe in that potential not just for the people who already know us, but for people on the outside as well.

To be successful, we have to embrace evangelism. We have to be willing to expose our passion and try—however we can—to make it attractive and relevant to others. We have to be curious and humble as we learn more about the people on the outside. We have to be willing to build doors and renovate rooms despite our prior attachments. We have to accept failures and keep pushing and dreaming forward. When we are open to what our communities of interest seek and honest about changing our work to meet them, we can build relevance.

We are missionaries. We are apostles. We do this work because it is big and important. It may not be hot. It may not be trending. But it can be relevant to the people we care about. It's our job—our glorious opportunity—to make it so.

A GREAT TREASURE

Imagine you are entrusted with a great treasure. A stunning painting. A perfect aria. A pristine waterfall. The word of God.

You want to protect the treasure, so you wrap it in ritual and reverence. You put it in a room that is only open to the public during working hours. In a performance hall with perfect acoustics, where tickets cost hundreds of dollars. At the end of a trail only accessible by foot, miles from the nearest parking lot. In a shroud of rhetoric and rules about when to stand and when to sit and what hat to wear.

These rituals give the treasure power, but they also block direct access to it. Over time, treasure-keepers become more and more invested in the rituals around the treasure, believing that the rituals not only keep the treasure safe but provide the one true way to experience it. To take the treasure out of the wrapper would be dangerous and a fundamental distortion of its value.

The treasure becomes like a mummy deep in a crypt, bound and gagged by its protectors. Silenced. Deadened. Regular people see the locked door but not the shining glory within. The rhetoric around the treasure gets bulkier, its light dimmer. People stop caring that there was something powerful there in the first place. Hand them a treasure map, and they throw it out. Too much work. Too expensive. Not for me. Not worth it.

Relevance is about making it worth it. Flinging open the door to the treasure. Bringing darkness into light.

What does it feel like to unlock that door? To find out, practice empathy. Put yourself in the shoes of the outsider beyond the door.

Imagine yourself outside the door, unaware that it exists. Someone hands you a key and says, "this is a key to a room that holds a great treasure."

You ask: "what's the treasure? Gold? Inner peace? The world's best pad thai?"

She replies: "I cannot tell you."

You put the key in your pocket. Maybe someday you'll use it. Maybe never.

Now imagine someone asks you: "What do you value most in this world?"

You think about it. You gather the courage. You answer honestly.

And then she says, "I know of a room that holds a treasure that speaks to that thing you most value. Here is how the treasure enhances your values. Here is a key to the door to that treasure."

What do you do now?

INDEX OF PROJECTS AND PLACES

S

T

W

Y

ACKNOWLEDGEMENTS

Thank you for joining me on this quest for relevance. This book was a pleasure to write, a learning journey that challenged and inspired me. I experienced a lot of positive cognitive effect as I wrote it (accompanied by plenty of effort).

I am especially grateful to Elise Granata, who served as lead content reviewer, editor, and cheerleader-in-chief. Elise also designed the beautiful cover and interior of this book. I thank Jon Moscone for writing the preface—several prefaces by the time we finished—and lending his considerable experience and reputation to help make this book relevant to people beyond my world. I greatly appreciate the James Irvine Foundation, which provided a grant to help support this book's development. My colleagues at the Irvine Foundation—Josephine Ramirez, Ted Russell, and Jeanne Sakamoto—are fiercely dedicated to making the arts matter to more people. They are fighting battles for relevance in the field of philanthropy, and they inspire me.

The great pleasure of this work was the opportunity to learn as I wrote. I didn't start with a thesis but rather with a set of questions I eagerly explored with the help of expert guides. Bill Ladusaw gave me a crash course in linguistics and the academic study of relevance. Monica Montgomery helped me learn more about issues of relevance and cultural appropriation around the #BlackLivesMatter movement. Adam Boal, Alexandra Fitzsimmons, Drew Himmelstein, Kemi Ilesanmi, Jon Moscone, and Whitney Smith turned me onto stunning examples I never would have found on my own. And everyone profiled in the book gave generously of their time in interviews, fact-checking, and thoughtful discussion about their work.

Thanks too to Museum 2.0 readers for giving me the space to write this book. While I never asked your permission directly, this book was only possible because I broke my nine-year streak of weekly blog posts to make space to write it. Even when I was afraid I might let you down, you believed in me and encouraged me on this path.

I am especially grateful to everyone who read the open call for case studies on the Museum 2.0 blog and took the time to share a story with me. There were several people who submitted stories of relevance that could not make it into the book for any number of reasons. I hope you will keep sharing your stories at **www.artofrelevance.org**. It's a good thing that we work in a world where there are too many relevant examples to fit them all in one book.

The content reviewers for this book were both brutally honest and terrifically supportive. Thank you to Jasmin Avila, Hannah Fox, Elise Granata, Porchia Moore, Ian David Moss, Devon Smith, Mimosa Shah, Beck Tench, Kevin Von Appen, Bruce Wyman, and Laura Zabel for making this book better.

I couldn't have written this book without my family. My mom Sarina and husband Sibley both did close reads on the final draft, deftly making it better. Sibley graciously gave me the space to write, whisking our toddler out of the house when necessary. My sister Morgan was writing a book at the same time, and we encouraged each other on our parallel journeys. My dad, Scott, allowed himself to be turned into a case study. They are all amazing and I'm lucky to have them.

Finally, I want to thank the incredible staff and board members with whom I work at the Santa Cruz Museum of Art & History. I have learned so much about relevance from and alongside you. Every day, I am amazed anew at how you strive for relevance, confront its challenges, and make it shine. You inspire me to keep working and dreaming with our diverse community. Thank you.

ABOUT THE AUTHOR

NINA SIMON has been described as a "museum visionary" by Smithsonian Magazine for her audience-centered approach to design. She has consulted with hundreds of international museums, libraries, parks, historic sites, art and cultural centers on issues of relevance, community engagement, and participatory design. Nina is the author of the best-selling book The Participatory Museum and the popular Museum 2.0 blog. Her work has been shared in the Wall Street Journal, New York Times, NPR, and TEDx. She lives off the grid in the Santa Cruz mountains with fourteen people, twenty-seven chickens, five dogs, and one zipline.

Made in the USA
San Bernardino, CA
14 May 2018